The Other Wing

A MEMOIR

Captain Bob Warinner

A PRAYER OF GRATITUDE

"Dear Father, I come to you in Jesus' name acknowledging that all I have comes from you. I know joy because of your love. I know grace because of your forgiveness. I know peace because of your promises. I know hope because of your eminent return. All I have, all I am, and all I've accomplished is because of you. Thank you for what you have done for me—what you continue to do in my life—what you are about to do for me! I stand in awe of your blessings, firmly grounded in gratitude for the ways you care for me. I love you Lord! Thank you!"

ISBN: 978-1-7376384-6-9

Published by
The Old Paths Publications
www.theoldpathspublications.com
TOP@theoldpathspublications.com
12/30/2021

Copyright © 2021 Robert Warinner
All rights reserved.

Praise the Savior, Ye Who Know Him!

Praise the Savior, ye who know Him!
Who can tell how much we owe Him?
Gladly let us render to Him
All we are and have.

Jesus is the Name that charms us,
He for conflicts fits and arms us;
Nothing moves and nothing harms us
When we trust in Him.

Trust in Him, ye saints, forever;
He is faithful, changing never;
Neither force nor guile can sever
Those He loves from Him.

Keep us, Lord, O, keep us cleaving
To Thyself and still believing.
Till the hour of our receiving
Promised joys with Thee.

Then we shall be where we would be,
Then we shall be what we should be;
Things which are not now, nor could be,
Soon shall be our own.
—*Thomas Kelly*

*Dedicated to my father, Royal Henry Warinner,
who loved aviation and instilled in his boys the desire to take to the air;
and to my oldest brother, Larry Leroy Warinner,
who taught each of his younger brothers to fly and without whom
I may never have had the privilege of living this story.*

Contents

    Forward 9
    Preface 11
1. Farm Years 13
2. Hitchhikes and Hijinx 25
3. New Relationships 33
4. Frontier Airlines 37
5. American Dream 45
6. Changes 53
7. Wings As Eagles Mission Air Service 63
8. Wings Aloft 69
9. Learning to Trust 75
10. Beyond Our Horizon 81
11. Over Mountain and Jungle 85
12. Down Under 109
13. God Builds a Team 121
14. Central America 127
15. Mission Field Hardships 137
16. Road Trip 145
17. Never Quit 149
18. Mercy Flight 163
19. Enlarging Our Coasts 169
20. The Mighty Hand of God 185
21. A Table in the Wilderness 189
22. To the Work 199
23. Trust in Him 207
24. A New Role 211
    Epilogue 215
    Appendix A: Heaven or Hell? 217
    Appendix B: Letters 219
    Appendix C: WAE Trip History 223
    WAE info 233
    Acknowledgements 235

Foreword

"For my thoughts are not your thoughts, neither are your ways my ways, saith the LORD. *For as the heavens are higher than the earth, so are my ways higher than your ways, and my thoughts than your thoughts."*—Isaiah 55:8–9

Our sovereign, omniscient God works in wonderful and marvelous ways to bring about his will in the lives of his servants. When the Lord brought Brother Bob Warinner to Park Rapids, Minnesota, and to First Baptist Church, where I was pastor, I was very pleased for two reasons. First, I believe that every pastor feels blessed with the arrival of a new, Biblically-grounded family ready to participate in the local church ministry. That was the case with the Warinner family.

The second reason is a much more personal one. Bob was a commercial airline pilot, and I had a very special interest in aviation. When I graduated from Bible school, I desired to serve the Lord in the field of missionary aviation, but the Lord closed that door. However, since I was a licensed aircraft mechanic, God did allow me to work for a number of years for the Flying Tiger Line, an airline started after World War II by the members of the American volunteer group that had served in China and had become the famous Flying Tigers. During those years of working personally and professionally with those pilot heroes, I grew to love flying, and my life pretty much revolved around airplanes.

Many years later when I was a pastor and Brother Warinner invited me to fly with him, I did not even think twice before answering yes. I flew with him on a number of occasions as part of the church outreach as the Lord was enlarging my ministry vision, especially in the area of producing Scripture portions to send to people in other countries and cultures who did not have access to Bibles in their native languages. That eventually led to my first foreign mission trip with Brother Warinner in April 1985. I thought that trip was made to deliver about a thousand Scripture portions (John and Romans booklets) in Spanish to Veracruz, Mexico, but I had no idea what the Lord was about to do in my life.

The day after we flew into Mexico, after driving to the end of the road in the mountains northwest of Veracruz, each of us men carried a box of Scriptures on our shoulders up through the coffee trees growing on the mountainside to finally reach the Totonac Indian village late in the day. For many hours we went from home to home, where missionary Don Rogers helped the people with their spiritual needs. During that time, I began to realize that the Lord had brought me there to impress upon me the great need for the gospel in Mexico. That trip changed my life and eventually led to more than thirty years of church planting and pastor-mentoring in Mexico. My eyes certainly did affect my heart (Lamentations 3:51a) during those days in Mexico.

It is my prayer that as you read this book the Lord will open your eyes and your heart to the great need for the Word of God around the world and that you will be divinely inspired to follow God's leading for your life, whatever and wherever that may be.

—Missionary Warren Klenk

Preface

As I look back on my life now, it all seems almost impossible. I was on a long road trip with several men from Oshkosh, Wisconsin, to Prince Albert, Saskatchewan, to receive a damaged aircraft that had been donated to our ministry. We began talking as friends do on long drives, sharing stories of the past and how, by God's grace, things had come to be.

"You should write a book!" one of the men said.

This was not the first time that thought had entered my mind. After praying and asking the Lord whether I should write my memoirs, the suggestion to share my life story continued to press on my heart, and the Lord would not let me rest. As I contemplate the miraculous working of the Lord over these past eighty-three years, I stand in awe of God's mercy and grace, that he would choose me from such humble beginnings to serve him. I was just a boy from Minnesota who wanted to fly airplanes. And for God to use me to launch the Wings As Eagles Mission Air Service, and for it to prosper, expand, and continue functioning for the glory of God, thirty-six years later, is nothing short of a miracle by a mighty God!

These past thirty-six years in the Wings ministry have been the happiest, most fulfilling years of our lives. I have learned that obedience brings blessing, and disobedience brings conflict! "*. . . blessed are they that hear the word of God, and keep it*" (Luke 11:28).

Only God could orchestrate the events that created *Wings As Eagles*. My heart's desire is that the story in this book might touch the hearts of its readers for the glory of God and perhaps encourage others, especially young men, to say, "Here am I, Lord, send me!" This is the place where God had to bring me in order for the birth of the ministry to occur.

My story is by no means a blueprint for others, but it offers proof that God can use anyone at any point in life to bring about his purposes and further his work on earth. May God, through these pages, bless your heart, challenge you, and encourage you to surrender to the mission he has created specifically for you.

1

Farm Years

"Before I formed thee in the belly I knew thee........"—*Jeremiah 1:5*

My life began in 1937, in a little, brown, two-story house in the small town of Cushing, Minnesota, the seventh child of what would be a family of ten children. My dad, Royal Henry Warinner, was born in 1904 on the family farm in the same house where I would spend most of my first ten years. His parents were of mixed German descent and had moved to Minnesota from Kentucky in the 1890s. My mother, Lorraine Geraldine Stahlhandske, was born in 1910 and raised in the town of Staples, Minnesota, twelve miles northwest of the farm. Her father was a railroad train engineer, and her family was of mixed Swedish descent. I guess that makes me a Heinz 57!

Our family lived on a 120-acre farm located about one mile north of Lincoln, Minnesota. The quarter-mile driveway led south to a small farmhouse and barn. Along the west side of the driveway was a beautiful stand of white pine trees. Along the east side was an eleven-acre hay field that Dad used as a landing strip. To the west of the house a hand pump near the barn supplied the water. (I once tried to lick the frost off that pump and quickly wished I hadn't!) Farther down the slope the land turned into swamp. The acreage behind and south of the house was heavily wooded with a beautiful stream flowing through a meadow across the southwest corner.

When I was about six months old, my older brother Ronnie, who was two years old, fell into a copper tub of scalding water that our mother had prepared for washing clothes and received third degree burns over his entire body. He died shortly after arriving at the nearest hospital in Little Falls. Although this tragedy in our home ultimately left our family with only nine children, my Christian parents had a deep faith in the Lord, which carried them through this profound heartbreak in their lives.

My birthplace in Cushing, Minnesota

At the time I was born, my dad owned a garage in Cushing and sold new Fords, but he also loved and was learning to fly airplanes. His heart eventually turned from auto sales and repair to aviation. He obtained his private pilot's certificate and earned his airframe and powerplant mechanics license (A&P). By 1939, when I was a little over a year old, Dad accepted a job as an aircraft mechanic at the airport in Robbinsdale, Minnesota. He sold the home and business in Cushing, and moved us about five miles north to the family farm. He commuted, flying his own airplane from the farm to work, coming home only on weekends. By the time I was five years old Dad had purchased a straight-wing Stinson, a five-place aircraft. He later bought and rebuilt a Waco UPF-7, which was a three-place, open-cockpit biplane. As a pilot and aircraft owner, he was well-known around our area and did a lot of barnstorm-type flying, giving rides from a hay field at our farm and at farms and smaller airports throughout northern Minnesota on weekends.

Dad was also a lay preacher and often filled the pulpit in the absence of the pastor. When he was home, he faithfully led the family in Bible devotions. Our whole family regularly attended the Church of Christ in Philbrook, Minnesota, a little burg about five miles northwest of our farm. Those years on the farm were happy years, although difficult, as it was during World War II.

Dad was a man of prayer, and he taught us the importance of prayer. My earliest memory of answered prayer took place shortly after Dad had purchased a new pair of shoes for me. On the farm we often went barefoot. I had taken off my new shoes and was running around outside when Dad asked me, "Where are your new shoes?" I had forgotten where I had left them.

"I don't know," I told him.

"You had better find those shoes!" Dad said. When my dad spoke, he meant business. I cried out to the Lord as a five-year-old boy, and immediately the thought came to my mind as to their location. I went to the garage where the Lord had told me to go, and there they were. That first recollection of answered prayer made an impression on me that I never forgot.

In the early days on the farm we had no electricity, so our lighting was strictly candles and kerosene lamps. Dad was an ambitious, innovative man, and he later built a garage, where he installed a homebuilt, gas-powered generator that he hooked up to supply electricity to the house. A week or two before Christmas in 1944, a short in the "light plant" system apparently developed, causing the generator to catch fire, and burning the garage to the ground. Mother and Dad had stored many Christmas presents they had purchased for the family in the garage, and of course all the presents burned with it, leaving the Christmas of 1944 a rather slim one, to say the least.

One interesting thing that came out of the garage fire, at least for me, was the fishing spear that I found when I was digging through the rubble and charred mess that emerged from the melted snow the following spring. I salvaged the spear and attached a broom handle to it. My brother Bill, a neighborhood friend Howard, and I decided to go fishing in the stream that flowed through our back forty, so we made our way to a place where the road crossed the stream. I climbed up the bank and stood on the bridge looking down into the stream, holding my spear. When I saw what looked like a fish, I threw the spear and ended up spearing a sucker that was at least eight pounds and probably about two feet long. It was so heavy that Bill had to help me pull it out. Bill put a stake through its gills, and Howard and I hauled it all the way back home, about a mile down the gravel road and then through the woods, with its tail dragging on the ground. Since our fishing and hunting often provided the meat for our meals, that fish fed the family for at least one meal. Our family ate lots of fish back in those days. The water was good, clear, clean water, and the suckerfish didn't taste bad, especially to hungry children!

Dad and Mom in front of the Stinson aircraft he had purchased

In March of 1945 the youngest member of our family, eight-month-old Gloria, contracted viral pneumonia. We were 12 miles from the nearest hospital, and we were snowed in at the farm. Since our driveway was about a quarter of a mile long and the snow was up to our hips, there was no way we could dig ourselves out. Mother cranked the wall phone and called Dad, who was at work in Robbinsdale, and asked him to fly home and then fly her and Gloria to the hospital. The morning was sunny and clear, while we waited for Dad to arrive in the J-3 Cub on skis. The sun climbed and slowly began its circle above the snow-white fields. Afternoon came, and Dad still had not arrived. In a J-3 Cub, even from Minneapolis, it was only an hour's flight, at the very most two hours. So Mother cranked the phone and called again.

"Mabel!" she said to the operator, "Would you ring the airport at Robbinsdale, Minnesota?" She paused, waiting to be put through to the airport, and upon getting someone to answer, she asked, "Has Royal Warinner left yet?"

"Oh yes," she was told. "He left early this morning."

We waited.

Mother called again. Still no report from Dad. Around four o'clock that afternoon with the sun setting, Dad's sister Aunt Mary and a friend from Cushing came walking up the driveway through the snow. They gave us the horrific news that my dad had been killed that morning in a midair collision. I'm sure that was what Mother had feared throughout the day that she would hear, and I remember her breaking into tears and crying uncontrollably for some time. In the hours that followed, Gloria was taken to the hospital by Aunt Mary and eventually made a full recovery.

Dad had taken to the air that day around 6 or 7 a.m. About the same time a student pilot took off for a practice flight, also in a Piper J-3, and decided to have a little fun with Dad. Catching up to him over Osseo, about ten miles from the airport, he dove under Dad's aircraft, apparently intending to come up in front of him to give him a scare. Misjudging, the student pilot caught the vertical fin of his tail section on Dad's right-wing tip and tore it out of its attachment point, causing Dad to spin out of control and crash, killing him instantly. Of course, anxiously waiting at home, we knew nothing of the accident until late in the afternoon. Our lives would change dramatically from that point on.

At the time of Dad's death, I was seven years old, and it was decided that the younger children, Gloria, Doug, Rosalie, and I, would not attend the funeral. Since I had last seen Dad alive and well, I would look for him expectantly when we went to town or other places in the area. I struggled with this searching for him until I was in my late teens. I believe my not seeing him at the funeral failed to bring reality and finality to my mind.

Life insurance was uncommon in those days, and unfortunately Dad didn't have any. It wasn't long before Mother was forced to go to work, leaving us on the farm either with sitters or to care for ourselves. At times it was all mayhem: tempers flared often, and sometimes butcher knives and pitchforks were brandished. It is only by the grace of God that we survived those days and grew up actually loving one another!

Things were tough on the farm without Dad. Late one winter evening Mother was on her way home from Motley, Minnesota, where she worked as a waitress. She had parked her car at a neighbor's place because our driveway was blocked with snow and began to walk through the fields to our house. The snow was knee-deep, as it was a cold, blizzardy night. She became very cold and tired and began to feel extremely sleepy. She believes she was close to freezing to death when she looked up and, in the distance, saw a dim light in our house. She was filled with the realization that the nine children in that house were all depending on her. God, in his mercy and grace, gave her the will and strength to continue and to make it to the house safely.

Dad's brother, Uncle George Warinner, from whom I get my middle name, was a Wesleyan Methodist pastor in the little town of Beebe, South Dakota, west of Aberdeen. Uncle George invited me to spend a couple of summers with him after Dad died. There is no doubt that God used him in my life. I believe our time together had a profound effect on the man I would eventually become. I give much credit for my caring about the things of God to Uncle George's godly influence and prayers.

Uncle George Warinner

We had a piano in our home, and my mother often played the piano for church services. My sister Bette learned to play the piano by ear, and in the evening she would often sit in the dark and play gospel hymns while the family stood around her and sang. I believe the message of those hymns and the atmosphere created by Bette's playing also contributed greatly to the man I would become, especially developing my love for good gospel music.

Without a father, we all had to pick up our share of the load to keep things going on the farm. The boys were mainly responsible for the outside chores and duties, which included hauling water up the hill from the pump for cooking, bathing, and washing clothes. Mother washed clothes with a scrub board and a hand-cranked wringer. Later she got a washing machine with a gas-powered Briggs & Stratton motor, which eased the laundry chore considerably. Since water had to be carried from a hand pump down the hill, the family took baths once a week, and we all used the same water, beginning with the oldest first. The water in the tub turned black, as one by one, nine active children who had gone barefoot all week took their baths.

I did not have a toothbrush as a young boy; I cleaned my teeth with my fingernails. My first trip to the dentist was in my early teens, and I had at least 15 cavities. An old military dentist did the drilling and filling without freezing, painkillers, or drill coolant. The drill got hot and smelled, and I was in constant pain.

Other responsibilities we had as boys were milking the one or two cows that we had at the time and harvesting wood for the furnace. There was a big square register between the dining room and the living room that furnished heat for the entire house. The house was not large but had a basement, as well as first and second floors. There were three small bedrooms upstairs; one was used for storage, and the other two for girls' and boys' sleeping. We did not all have separate beds, so we had to share, often with a purring cat as well. My younger brother Doug and I were bed partners, and we frequently disagreed with each other, especially when we awakened earlier than perhaps we should have. I remember one particular morning in early spring, while the snow was still on the ground, Doug and I began to have words and woke up my older brother Bill, who was not very happy with our brotherly spat.

"Bob and Doug are fighting again!" Bill called out to Mother.

"All right!" she responded. "I will take care of that when I get up!"

I knew what was coming, so I bailed out of bed, dressed up nice and warm, and left the house for the woods in the back forty. I managed to stay away from the house until late afternoon when I was getting too cold and hungry to stay out any longer, so I went back inside and parked myself by the heat register.

Bill saw me and told Mother, who was busy in the bathroom, and when she came out, she looked at me and said, "Okay, let's go!" which meant we were going to the basement for an old-fashioned whipping. Bill was sitting in the kitchen by the door leading to the basement, whittling on a piece of wood from an old orange crate. As I walked past him, I smiled.

"You won't be smiling when you come back up!" he said.

Down in the basement Mother took the broom handle that she often spanked us with and began her motherly act of disciplining her son who had misbehaved. Little did she know that in my youthful wisdom I had stuffed several heavy wool socks in the seat of my pants. She gave me several whacks, and when I didn't cry, she stopped and felt my bottom. Either not detecting the socks stuffed in my pants or choosing not to say anything, she gave me several more whacks, and when I didn't cry, she stopped. She excused me from the basement, and I walked back upstairs past Bill, of course smiling smugly at him. He was so disappointed!

Farm house where I spent my early years

We had a couple of workhorses on the farm named King and Queen that we also used for riding. When I was about ten years old, Bill and I rode the horses down to the mailbox. I was riding my horse without a saddle or bridle and just had a halter and clothes line rope for reins, when my horse decided it was time to go home. She started galloping for all she was worth, while I hung on with little or no control. She ran past the house and headed for the back forty, but the gate was closed. She locked all fours, and I took to the air, flying over the fence and landing on my stomach on the other side which knocked the wind out of me. I have always counted that as my first flying lesson, but a softer, more controlled landing would have been very welcome! A short time later those horses were sold for mink food, because we could not afford to feed them. My older brothers were gone, so it fell on me to hold the horses while the man who picked them up for the rendering plant shot them. I held tight and tried to be brave. It was around this time as well that the beautiful stand of white pine trees was sold to a lumber company to help with much-needed family finances.

The following summer in 1948, mother sold the farm and moved us to Staples, Minnesota, where her brother Gordon lived and worked as a railroad engineer. She found a job at a local restaurant as a cook to meet the family's needs. When school was out in the spring of 1950, I was 12, and Mother announced that we were moving to Oregon. Early in their marriage Dad and Mother had taken a trip to Oregon to visit relatives, where they fell in love with that part of the country, returning to Minnesota with the dream of someday moving to Oregon themselves. By the time I was 12, our sister Bette had married, and she and her husband, Chuck Cruse, had moved to Garibaldi, Oregon, where Chuck had found work at a local plywood mill. Their move gave Mother incentive to move west, as well as opportunity to fulfill the dream that she and Dad had held for many years.

My oldest brother Larry had also recently married and was employed at a small airport in Nisswa, Minnesota. Bill had grown up to become a rather artistic guy, and he had found work at a sign shop in Staples, Minnesota, so our initial move to Oregon consisted of the six remaining children, with Joanne the oldest at age 18. My sister Mary Lou had a boyfriend, Don, who would soon become her husband, and he couldn't stand to see her go, so he moved with us. He owned a 1937 Chevrolet, and Mom owned a 1937 Ford, which we used to make the move.

Uncle Gordon built us a trailer to transport our belongings, and when it was loaded it looked like something out of the movie *Grapes of Wrath*, with tires hanging off the sides and all our earthly possessions tied down with a tarp and ropes. It took us seven days to travel from Staples, Minnesota, to Garibaldi, Oregon, approximately 1600 miles. It was quite an adventure in those days, as there were no freeways. We had to cross several rivers on barges because bridges had not yet been constructed.

After we departed Staples, our first destination was Fargo, North Dakota, where Mother's sister Margaret lived. We spent the night at their home and headed west again the next morning. We made it to Valley City, North Dakota, where we stopped for lunch at a little restaurant. After lunch we all loaded up in the cars and headed west once again. After about ten miles of driving, one of the kids apparently had to go to the bathroom. Upon making our stop, we discovered that little six-year-old Gloria was missing.

The trailer was attached to the '37 Ford, so Don went back to Valley City in his Chevy, stopping at the restaurant once again, where he found Gloria well cared for and waiting for someone to come back for her. Once again, we were all back together, and continued our journey west.

Doug, Gloria, Rosalie, Mom, and me

Over the next several days we managed to make it all the way to Saltese, Montana. The little '37 Ford was struggling to pull the trailer through the mountains, so in Saltese, at the base of the mountain just before going over the Continental Divide, we stopped and had a trailer hitch mounted on Don's '37 Chevrolet. Then we loaded up again and headed up the Continental Divide. About halfway up the mountain the '37 Ford started to overheat, so we stopped to let it cool and get some water out of a nearby stream for the radiator, only to discover that my eight-year-old brother Doug had been left behind in Saltese.

Mother turned the Ford around and headed back to Saltese. A few miles out of town she saw a pickup truck approaching with arms waving out both sides. Doug had failed to get back in the car in Saltese when we had the trailer hitch mounted, and when he realized he was left behind he got onto the highway and began to hitchhike. When a man in a pickup stopped and asked him where he was going, Doug told him he was going to Oregon—where in Oregon exactly he did not know—but that he had been left behind. The guy in the pickup was obviously trying to catch up to us and hoped that Doug would recognize the vehicles, just as he had.

All back together again, we continued the trip west. By the time we arrived in Coeur d'Alene, Idaho, Mother and Don had spent their last penny. Mom managed to send a wire to Bette's husband Chuck Cruse, who wired her $100 for us to complete the trip. Finally arriving in Garibaldi, Oregon, stone broke, we stayed with relatives for a short time until we could rent a house in Manzanita Beach, Oregon. Mother found a job as a cook; Don began work at a cheese factory; Joanne got a job as a waitress at a local restaurant; and the rest of us got acquainted with our new surroundings. We later moved to Salem, where all of us older kids got involved in harvesting crops like strawberries, string beans, cherries, and other produce, which helped meet our family's needs.

Our family shortly after our move to Oregon
Back row: Bill, Larry, Joanne, and Mary Lou
Front row: Rosalie, Bette, Gloria, Mom, Bob, and Doug

2

Hitchhikes and Hijinx

". . . thou understandest my thought afar off . . . and art acquainted with all my ways."—Psalm 139: 2–3

When Larry was 15, he had gotten a job at the Staples airport in Minnesota as a line boy and soon learned to fly. Seven years older than I, he was pretty well established in his flying when I was old enough and ready to learn. By the time we made our move to Oregon, Larry had obtained his commercial pilot license and was flying for John Reidl at Heywood Gull Lake Airport in Nisswa, Minnesota.

In the spring of 1952, when we had been in Oregon for two years and I was 14, my mother gave me five dollars and a package of diet pills to keep me from getting too hungry, and sent me off with her blessing to hitchhike my way about 1700 miles to Nisswa, Minnesota, to join my brother Larry, whom I had not seen for about a year. I had a small, cream-colored suitcase with Brainerd, Minnesota, printed on it in red letters, and, like all hitchhikers, I would extend my arm with my thumb up, asking for a ride whenever I saw a vehicle approaching. My first ride took me as far as Oregon City, just south of Portland, where I was dropped off. Then along came the Oregon State Patrol and picked me up, thinking I was a runaway. After talking to the patrolman for some time, I was able to convince him that I was traveling with parental permission. He allowed me to continue hitchhiking, but advised me not to put out my arm with my thumb up, telling me that that was against the law in the state of Oregon.

As I continued on my way, somewhere west of Coeur d'Alene, Idaho, with the sun setting, I was standing along the highway with my thumb out when a car came weaving down the highway. It veered over to my side and stopped to pick me up. The man driving had just been discharged from the Navy and had been drinking a lot, but I badly wanted a ride, so I foolishly got in with him. We drove only a short distance before we came to a bar, where he stopped to get more beer. Somehow I convinced him to let me drive. I had no driver's license, of course, but he didn't ask, so I drove through the night, and somewhere in eastern North Dakota he got upset with me for some reason and made me stop and get out. By God's grace, I had made it safely that far!

Later on, when I had been standing alongside the road for some time waiting for a ride and getting a little bored, I took out my pocket knife and began to whittle on a piece of wood I had found. As I was whittling, I cut myself, so I walked a short distance back to the nearest town, found a drugstore, and bought some Band-Aids. I patched myself up and went back to the highway to continue hitchhiking toward where my brother Larry lived in Nisswa. The Lord watched over me and blessed me with rides that took me through the nights and eventually to my destination. Arriving about three days later at the airport where Larry worked, I was very excited to see Larry again and also to be starting my very first job.

Because my little suitcase didn't hold much, my mother had promised to ship additional clothing to me, but approximately two weeks after arriving in Nisswa, I still had not received a box of clothing. Long distance calls were expensive, and I did not have the resources, so I came up with the idea to make a person-to-person call to Bob Clothes. Fortunately, Mother answered the phone, and of course there was no Bob Clothes present; however, she understood my message, and within a short time I received the additional clothing that I needed. In Nisswa I was hired as a line boy at the same airport as Larry, and he began to teach me to fly. My pay was ten dollars per week plus one hour of flying time. A golf driving range crossed the north-south grass strip, and we stored golf balls and other supplies in a small storage shed nearby, where I made myself comfortable with a single bed, washbasin, and hotplate, cooking my own meals, mostly canned pork and beans, which I love, and taking baths now and then in a nearby lake.

At season's end 1952 I stayed with Larry and his wife in Nisswa and attended school in Brainerd. All was going well, and the next summer in July when I was 15, early one beautiful morning when Larry was giving me flight instruction, he decided to let me solo. He had given me about 20 hours of instruction by this time and felt I was plenty capable. So he took a chance and soloed me at age 15, in spite of the fact that the minimum legal age was and is still 16. I successfully made three takeoffs and landings and then parked at our little terminal building. Just as I was getting out of the J-3 Cub, our boss John Reidl pulled up a little earlier than usual. My heart pounded, but I tried to look as casual as possible. He didn't seem to detect that anything unusual had gone on. Both Larry and I had come close to being in deep trouble! I swallowed hard and got on with my day, but things would never be quite the same again. I had successfully soloed at age 15, and I was filled with excitement, for I was more than likely the youngest solo pilot in the country at that moment.

Golf club house where we sold buckets of balls and where I lived

A wealthy family from Tulsa, Oklahoma, which owned a beautiful home on Gull Lake, used to fly into the Nisswa airport with a De Havilland Dove. In the fall of 1953 the elder son Jimmy took an interest in me and helped me financially, enabling me to return to Oregon for the school year. Jimmy, through the Rotary Club, would send me 120 dollars per month, which at that time allowed me to rent a small room with a kitchenette, where I lived by myself, cooked my own meals, and attended school. My mother and my siblings, who were living about seven miles away from my lodgings, helped me by doing my laundry. When school was out the next spring, I hitchhiked my way back to Nisswa and took up my job at Heywood Gull Lake Airport with Larry once again.

In February of 1955, when I was 17, I joined the Naval Air Reserve. I felt pretty important in my Navy uniform. When school ended in the spring and it was time to return to my job in Nisswa, I was ordered to go on a training cruise for the Navy. I went to my commander and told him that I couldn't go on the cruise because I had a job in Minnesota. The commander looked at me and said,

"You have two choices. You can either go on the cruise or go inactive." So I chose to go inactive, and that was the end of my military career.

That spring I purchased a '47 Ford, which I drove back to Nisswa for the summer. I continued to enjoy working at Heywood Gull Lake Airport, being with my brother Larry, and learning to fly. Our boss John Reidl had a contract with Minnesota Power and Light Company, flying the power lines to check for broken insulators, tree limbs across power lines, or any other problems. Larry was trained for this and given the responsibility of flying power line patrol, mostly in a 135 hp Piper Super Cub. I often had the awesome privilege of flying with Larry, which allowed me to gain both flying time and experience, as Larry allowed me to do a good share of the flying.

By this time, I had accumulated enough flight time and instruction to take my private pilot flight test. My boss signed my recommendation for the private pilot test, and I flew to Grand Rapids, Minnesota, where I took the flight test and failed the cross-country flight portion. I was disappointed in myself, but I flew back to Nisswa, where Larry gave me additional cross-country training, after which I returned to Grand Rapids and completed the flight test, receiving my private pilot license. I was so excited, and for sure I was one of the youngest private pilots in the country at that time.

Larry and Super Cub in 1953

For the most part my life was going pretty well, and by God's wonderful mercy and grace I managed to stay out of serious trouble. I was learning a lot and becoming quite self-sufficient. In retrospect, I'm so thankful that God has promised to be a father to the fatherless, and I can certainly see how I experienced his love and watch-care in my life, even though I had not yet given my life to Christ.

One afternoon Larry and John left me alone to tend to the golf driving range and any aircraft that came in. Three men in their late 20s or early 30s stopped in to drive a few golf balls. I sold them each a bucket of balls, but as they knocked them out, they would go out and pick up others, which of course was against the rules. I got after them for it, and one of the men came to the counter and reached across to grab me. I gave him my fist in the nose, and he began to bleed, which slowed him down a little. When the biggest of the three came after me, I took off running with a golf club in my hand. I stopped for a moment, ready to wrap that golf club around his head and then thought better of it and instead ran to our small administration building, where I locked the doors and immediately called the police. The police arrived quickly, as did Larry and John, and the men were dealt with. They took their bleeding friend to the hospital, and we discovered later that I had broken the man's nose.

One of the men returned a few days later to apologize, and he admitted that they had been drinking, had gone out for a drive, and had been smashing mailboxes along the highway. I have often reflected on God's wonderful hand of protection that was upon me in many ways all down through the years.

On my way back to Salem, Oregon, in the fall for school, I was driving just east of Billings, Montana, when I got pounded by a big thunderstorm with hail stones the size of baseballs. My car was dented all over; the windshield was cracked; and my spirit was a little damaged, but I continued on my way and made it safely back to Salem.

That school year when my sister Rosalie and I had dates, we both met up at a basketball game in a nearby town. Before we went in to watch the game, we parked next to each other and, as immature young men sometimes do, we decided to test our exhaust pipes to see whose was the loudest. Rosalie's friend and I were both revving the engines when a policeman tapped on my window. I took my foot off the gas immediately.

"Who has the loudest pipes?" the policeman asked me, not amused.

"I guess I do," I said sheepishly.

"Come with me," he said, and he took me to the local judge to be charged and pay a fine.

Of course, I had no money, but I did have a wristwatch, so the judge took my watch for security, told me to get the pipes fixed, and directed me to return to court on a certain date. Sometime between that night and my court date, I was again acting foolishly and drag racing in Salem when I broke the car's right rear axle. I forget how I got my car home that night, but when I later appeared in court, the judge asked me, "Did you get the pipes taken care of?"

"No," I said. "I broke an axle, and the car isn't driveable."

"Well, that's one way to fix it," he replied.

It cost my poor mother, who had taken me to the courthouse, 20 dollars because I was broke as usual and could not pay my fine. My watch was returned to me and I returned home with a mother who was not exactly pleased.

The next summer I left my job in Nisswa, moved to a job at the Brainerd, Minnesota airport, and joined the Civil Air Patrol. The Civil

Air Patrol also had a J-3 Cub, the same type aircraft I had soloed in and my dad was killed in. I was allowed to fly the J-3 for about three dollars per hour including gas. I flew the J-3 as much as I could afford. I enjoyed working at the Brainerd Airport and seemed to get along quite well with my employer, Dale Newberg. I kept busy mowing grass on airport property, fueling airplanes, and also performing aircraft maintenance under Dale's tutelage.

One day Dale asked me to take an Aeronca Champ and fly a man to Grand Rapids, Minnesota. He instructed me to be sure to check the oil before leaving Grand Rapids, because the neck of the oil tank was slightly cracked and leaked a little. We landed in Grand Rapids, where I dropped off my passenger and took off on my return flight to Brainerd, forgetting to check the oil. I was flying low level and having a good time when the oil pressure began to drop. Instantly I remembered that I hadn't checked the oil before leaving Grand Rapids, so I started a climb to gain altitude in order to look for a place to make a forced landing before I had engine stoppage. Spotting a straight stretch on the highway below, although it was heavily wooded on both sides, I started a descent, lined up with the highway, and at about 50 feet spotted a power line going across the highway. I pulled up to miss the power line and landed on the other side.

Shortly after touching down I must have experienced a crosswind gust, and I went off the road to the left and through the ditch, severely damaging the left gear. The plane came to rest with the leading edge of the left wing about three inches from a large tree. I was a little shaken up but unhurt. I got out of the airplane, and soon a man in a vehicle came along and gave me a ride to the nearest town where I could get to a telephone. I called Dale and told him what had happened. He was not a happy camper, but he was grateful that I was not hurt and that the airplane was not damaged any worse. I told Dale my location, and he drove up with a flatbed truck to pick me up, disassemble and load the airplane onto the truck, and drive back to Brainerd. I was not fired, but I got a stern warning. I learned a great lesson that day without paying too big a price. My guardian angel was kept mighty busy watching out for me!

Now and then I continued to fly with Larry on power line patrol, which allowed me to build the time necessary for my commercial pilot certificate. The summer I was 18 I had accumulated enough flight time to take my commercial pilot check ride. John gave me the check ride, and this time I passed with flying colors, so to speak. In adding up my flight time in my log book, however, I was about five hours short of the required 200 hours for a commercial certificate, so, with John's blessing, I was given five hours of "P-51" time. In other words, the additional hours were added to my log book with an ink pen called a Parker 51 to show the 200 hours required. Here I was, just 18 years old with a commercial pilot license, proud of my accomplishments at such a young age and yet not sure where it was all going to lead.

Because Brainerd and Nisswa are resort areas, the business pretty well dies down after Labor Day. Shortly after my summer job at Brainerd ended, I decided not to return to Salem, but instead to move to Minneapolis, which was considerably closer to my brother Larry, and where some of Mother's family lived. There I enrolled in night school and started working in the tire installation department at Sears and Roebuck. Little did I know the many unbelievable ways the next three years would change my life, all for the better and all to the glory of God.

3

New Relationships

"But as many as received him, to them gave he power to become the sons of God, even to them that believe on his name."—John 1:12

I took a room at the old Wisconsin Hotel near downtown Minneapolis, across from the Lutheran Bible Institute. I met some of the students there, one of them being Dick Askvig, who became a dear friend and eventually asked me to room with him and another student. Some mutual friends invited me to attend a Lutheran church, but I was not comfortable with the liturgy and formality. My new friends, however, seeing my need for a personal relationship with Christ, had a genuine concern for me and witnessed to me. Some months later I was visiting in the area of Milaca, Minnesota, and before returning to Minneapolis decided to attend the evening service at the Evangelical Free Church in Milaca. God used the preaching that night to impress upon me the fact that I was lost and on my way to a devil's burning hell. I knew I desperately needed to trust Christ as my personal Savior. The preacher did not give an invitation to trust Christ, as is the custom in independent Baptist churches, so after the service I waited until everyone left and then I told the pastor that I needed to be saved. This self-assertiveness was a bold action on my part, for I was usually much more reserved. The pastor took me to his office and showed me some Scriptures, helping me to see my sinful condition and my need for salvation. As a result, on a Sunday evening in Novemberof 1956 I put my faith and trust in the finished work of Calvary. My interest in the things of God and the Word of God took a big leap forward.

"Therefore if any man be *in Christ,* he is *a new creature: old things are passed away; behold, all things are become new"* (2 Corinthians 5:17). Old things in my

life were passing away, and all things were becoming new, but my Christian growth was a very slow process. I had no one to disciple me and help me in my new relationship with Christ. During my lunch hours at Sears and Roebuck, I would go to the basement of the tire store where I could be alone and sit amongst the tires and read my Bible. No doubt this reading was a great help, but it was far from all I needed at the time. I began to attend an Evangelical Free Church close to the downtown Minneapolis area, but even there, no one took me under his wing to help me in my Christian growth, and I had neither the character nor the knowledge to accomplish it on my own. As a result, my spiritual growth was slow and difficult and filled with setbacks.

Before giving my heart to Christ, I had stolen a set of tires for a fellow employee in the tire shop who was planning a trip to Oregon for his vacation. Knowing that I was from Oregon, he had invited me to travel along with him and his wife. Before leaving on this trip, he made it known that he needed a new set of tires for his later model Ford and asked if I would help him secure them from the Sears inventory. I foolishly agreed. We made our trip to Oregon on the stolen tires and by God's undeserved mercy and grace we had a safe and uneventful trip. It was good to see Mom and other family again. However, not too long after our return to work my friend was found out and fired. Later that same afternoon, I was called into the store detective's office and questioned about the theft. I confessed and told the detective about my part and also that I had gotten saved and had not stolen anything since. He immediately wanted to know what I had been saved from. I told him that I had trusted Jesus Christ as my Savior and that he had saved me from hell. He was a little taken aback with that but told me he had to let me go. I was dismayed of course, but a short time later I found a job at a gas service station in North Minneapolis. I worked there until I acquired my flight instructor certificate and began flight instructing at Crystal Airport, located in a northwest suburb of Minneapolis. Many lessons for me came the hard way, but I learned here that my sins would indeed find me out!

One evening Dick Askvig and I attended a Youth for Christ rally at First Baptist Church in downtown Minneapolis. God was dealing with my heart, and when the invitation was given, I responded, surrendering to the call of missionary aviation. Shortly thereafter I came into possession of the book *Jungle Pilot*, which is the story of missionary Nate Saint and his martyrdom along with four other missionaries in their attempt to reach the Auca tribe in Ecuador with the gospel. God really spoke to me through that missionary story and began a work in my heart that would become a reality many years later.

Some months after attending the Youth for Christ rally, I decided to go roller-skating on a Saturday evening. When it was time for a couple's skate, I saw a pretty girl who I wanted to get acquainted with, so I asked her if she would skate with me. Her name was Juanita, and after the couple's skate, I bought her a Coke and asked for her phone number. She was a sweet, friendly, never-meets-a-stranger type, and she told me her number, thinking I would not be able to remember it. I repeated it in my mind and held it there long enough to write it in the dust of my windshield with my fingertip. The next day I called her and asked if she would like to go for an airplane ride, thinking this newly minted, commercial-rated pilot could really impress her. She agreed!

I rented a Piper PA-12, a tandem seating aircraft with pilot in front and passenger in back. The Lutheran church she attended with her parents was having a church picnic that afternoon west of Minneapolis near Lake Minnetonka. We flew out to the Lake Minnetonka area to find the picnic, where I circled several times, rocking my wings to say hello, and then I decided it was time to fly back to the airport in Crystal, Minnesota, where I had rented the aircraft. Without looking at the compass, I rolled out on a heading that I thought would take us back. After flying for several minutes, I realized that I should be seeing the city of Minneapolis, especially the tallest building, which at that time was the Foshay Tower. Seeing neither, I glanced at my compass and saw that I was going west when I should have been going east. Now my mental compass was really messed up! I made a right turn 180° and saw Minneapolis and the Foshay Tower on the distant horizon. But now, with my mental compass being 180° out of phase, I was confused as to where the airport was.

"Juanita?" I asked innocently, "Do you recognize anything out there?"

"Yes," she replied, pointing. "That's Miracle Mile Shopping Center, and my house is just over there a little way."

"Ah . . . and where do you think the airport would be?"

"Oh, it's up that way," she replied, pointing north, which in my mind was south. She thought I was giving her a little quiz, not desperately searching for directions.

Since I was still mixed up, I took her word and made a left turn, hoping that we really were then heading toward the airport. Once I made the turn and headed north, the compass in my brain finally settled down, and things went back to normal. We flew to the airport, where we made a normal landing, and everything ended safely, with Juanita none the wiser. She was impressed with our afternoon of flying, and I did not reveal the fact that I had gotten confused until many years later.

I continued to press forward with my flying, working toward a flight instructor certificate, attending ground school at the University of Minnesota in preparation for the written exam. Juanita and I spent many of our dates with my nose in the books while she quizzed me from the question-and-answer section. This activity helped her learn a lot about my life, about aviation, and about where I was heading. She seemed to love it, saying "I do" in marriage just eight months after our first flight together. We were married at Wooddale Lutheran Church in St. Louis Park, Minnesota, on February 8, 1958. God would greatly bless our marriage and our lives together, although the years would not be without some trials and tribulations.

Our wedding picture

4

Frontier Airlines

"For I know the thoughts that I think toward you, saith the LORD, thoughts of peace, and not of evil, to give you an expected end."—Jeremiah 29:11

Shortly after our marriage in February of 1958, at the age of 20, I successfully passed my flight instructor check ride, and that same month I began instructing in a Cessna-140 at South St. Paul Airport in St. Paul, Minnesota. Then in March I started instructing and flying some charter flights for Ford Aviation at Crystal Airport. Later, Larry, who was now flying for North Central Airlines, encouraged me to call and apply with Frontier Airlines out of Denver, Colorado, knowing that they were looking for pilots.

When I applied to Frontier Airlines, I had a total of 1250 hours of single engine time in various types of smaller aircraft, a commercial pilot license, an instrument rating, and the flight instructor rating. However, I had no multiengine time. When I called Johnny Myers, who was the chief pilot with Frontier Airlines at the time, I learned that Frontier required at least 500 hours of multiengine time before they would hire a pilot. However, when I told him I was only 21 years old, he said, "In that case, maybe we can do something for you," and arranged for me to fly to Denver for an interview.

I was hired by Frontier Airlines in June of 1959 and entered their training program, which included two weeks of classroom training and five hours of flight training in the right seat of the DC-3. After I completed their training program, I began flying as a copilot on Douglas DC-3s. Juanita and I moved to Omaha, Nebraska, where we rented a small apartment for 100 dollars per month.

The routes out of Omaha went west through Nebraska to Rapid City, South Dakota, and Denver, Colorado, and also south to St Joseph, Missouri, and Kansas City, Missouri. I will never forget how awestruck I was the first time I climbed into that large airplane and looked out at those big engines and large, long wings. No pun intended, but I was flying high for a 21year-old!

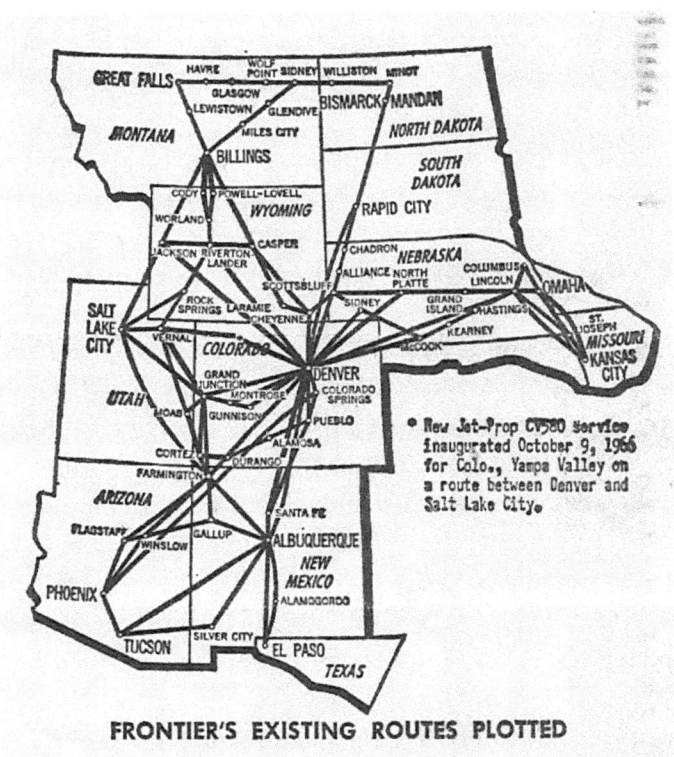

FRONTIER'S EXISTING ROUTES PLOTTED

Now and then I couldn't resist pulling a little prank on the captain I was flying with, if I were sure he had a sense of humor. In the early days of the airline business, the captain and copilot stayed in the same hotel room. One such time we had an overnight at the Corn Husker Hotel in Lincoln, Nebraska. That night I got to the room a few minutes before the captain. I got the wise idea to get into the closet and close the door. The captain entered the room and opened the closet door to hang up his uniform jacket as I had anticipated he would. When he did, I fell out at him like a corpse. He stepped back and yelped, then, realizing it was me, started to laugh, "Man you scared me half to death! I'm glad I have a strong heart." We fortunately had a good laugh together, but I never pulled that prank again.

As a result of being hired by Frontier Airlines, I was given a deferment by the military draft board. All airlines at that time had an agreement with the military that in the event of an all-out war, we would be absorbed into the military for transporting troops. After eight years of inactive service, I was issued an honorable discharge from the United States Navy in January of 1963.

After we moved to Omaha, Juanita and I started attending an Evangelical Free Church in Omaha and became good friends with the pastor and his wife. During this time Juanita became very ill. We went to several doctors, but they were unable to diagnose the problem. Our pastor's wife recommended her gynecologist to us, who, within the first 30 minutes of the appointment, diagnosed the issue as ovarian cysts. Juanita underwent an operation a short time later, and the doctor removed both ovaries and then transplanted a small piece of good flesh from one of the ovaries in their place. We were told at that time that this type of surgery was the first of its kind successfully performed in the United States. God indeed worked a miracle in our lives, one that would continue to unfold in his time.

We lived in Omaha until the summer of 1961, when I felt led to go to Bible college to prepare to serve the Lord in missionary aviation. I applied to a Bible college in Minneapolis, Minnesota, resigned my position with Frontier Airlines, and moved back to Minneapolis. Shortly thereafter we discovered the unexpected miracle of miracles in our lives—that we were expecting our first child. Of course we were thrilled with this development, but with a baby on the way, we just didn't see how we could make our plans work. Juanita and I were still in the early years of our marriage and barely making it financially. Our plan had been for Juanita to work full time while I went to school and worked part time, but that would be impossible with a baby on the way. What was more, I loved flying. In under a decade I had gone from flying little single-engine aircraft to flying multiengine passenger liners across the continent. I had a uniform, a flight bag, and the camaraderie of fellow crew members, lost souls as they were. I had turned my back on that for some noble but undefined cause, no income, and now the "complication" of a baby. There was no way this was all going to work out. So I called the school and told them I wouldn't be coming, and I began to look for a flying job in the Minneapolis area. As I look back, I can see God's gracious hand of protection upon us, working in our lives despite our apparent weakness and puny faith. I believe now that the school I had applied to was not the school that God would have had me attend, because of their doctrinal stand, but I had no ability to discern that at the time.

I started flying a Cessna-310 part time for a company called Sterner Industries. We were still only barely scraping by financially when my older brother Bill came to spend a day or two with us. All we had in the house for supper one night was my old standby, a can of pork and beans. It seems we could always count on having my favorite food on hand! We bowed our heads for prayer before our meal.

"Lord," I prayed, "Please bless these beans . . . " and we all laughed. *"Better is a dinner of herbs where love is........"* (Proverbs 15:17).

I knew I had to find a fulltime flying job again in order to meet our needs, so I applied to several companies to no avail. I had also reapplied to Frontier. Larry was still flying for North Central Airlines at that time, so he arranged for me to fly on a pass to go see him in Detroit, Michigan, where he was based. While I was in Green Bay, Wisconsin, for a short stop before continuing on to Detroit, I was summoned to the North Central ticket counter and told to call the Frontier chief pilot, John Myers. In short order I was hired back and told to report to Denver, Colorado, for training. In February of 1962 I returned to Frontier Airlines, where I would remain for the next 24 years.

In March of 1962 Juanita gave birth to a healthy baby boy we named Gary. My job allowed me to adequately provide for our family. I settled into airline flying and of course enjoyed it.

I was flying copilot on the Douglas DC-3 again, until a couple of years later when I checked out as a copilot on the Convair-340. The Convair-340s were converted at a later date to General Motors Allison turboprop Convair-580s, with a seating capacity of 53.

DC-3

Convair-580

In 1963 our family grew as our daughter Cynthia, or Cindy as we came to call her, was born in April of that year. We attended an Evangelical Free Church in Aurora, and it was there that I discovered that I had a singing voice and could carry a tune. A couple in the church, Gilbert and Dorothy Glad, played the piano and organ and ran the music program. We were new to the congregation, and as Gilbert heard me singing out during congregational singing, he soon asked if I would sing a solo in church. I was very nervous and felt self-conscious doing anything in front of a group so I told him no. But Gilbert wouldn't take no for an answer.

"Would you sing a duet with me on a Sunday morning?" he asked.
"No!"
Then it was, "How about in the evening service?"
"No!"
"We do a service at the Denver Rescue Mission . . . would you sing with me there? The drunks don't care!"
"Well . . . I might consider that."

Gilbert got me started singing at the first opportunity, and from there I began singing duets and trios, eventually a solo at the Rescue Mission. Then we repeated the process at church on Wednesdays, Sunday nights, Sunday mornings, and finally solos on a regular basis. I owe Gilbert and Dorothy Glad a great debt of gratitude for their work with me. Their patience literally changed my life and helped prepare me for the future God had in store for me.

My career with Frontier went quite smoothly and provided very well for a growing family, bringing with it some interesting experiences and personalities. In October of 1964 the movie *Cheyenne Autumn* was being produced. It is based on the historical event of the Trail of Tears, which took place when the Cheyenne Indian people left the Four Corners area of Arizona and walked the 1200 miles back to their homeland in Montana. The production crew chartered a Frontier DC-3 to fly several actors from Torrington, Wyoming, one of the movie sites, to Cheyenne, Wyoming, for the premiere showing of the film. The crew on that flight was yours truly and Captain Dave Kohler. We flew from Denver to Torrington empty, where we were transported to the set where film shooting had taken place, giving us an opportunity to observe and meet some of the actors. Upon returning to the airport for our trip to Cheyenne, we had on board celebrities Jimmy Stewart, Ricardo Montalban, Patrick Wayne, Karl Malden, Carroll Baker, and Mike Mazurki. En route to Cheyenne, Captain Kohler had me vacate the copilot seat so that Pat Wayne could take my seat and fly while I occupied the jump seat until approaching Cheyenne for landing!

In September of 1966 Frontier purchased a Boeing 727–100 aircraft, and by this time my seniority allowed me to bid for a 727 copilot position. I flew copilot on the 727–100 and later the 727–200 for a total of four years. In 1973 I checked out as a captain on the Convair-580.

THE OTHER WING

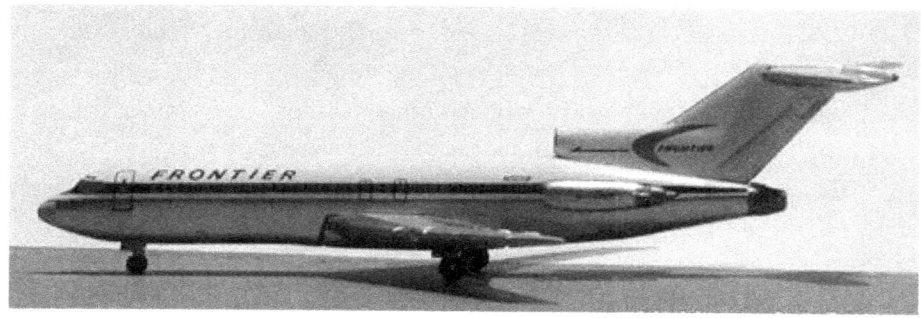

Boeing 727–100

One close call I had in my career with Frontier occurred while on an IFR (instrument flight rules), ILS (instrument landing system-a precision type approach) to runway 27 (runway heading of 270 degrees) into Cheyenne, Wyoming, in the 580, with the weather at minimums and a maximum tailwind component. The copilot was flying, and we missed the approach, so we pulled up and went around for a second approach. He was still a little left of course and still a couple hundred feet above minimums when we heard a loud noise and noticed an over-temp light on the left engine, with the left engine spooling down, indicating engine failure. I quickly took control and called for max power on the good engine and for gear retraction. We were down to VMC (velocity of minimum control) 90 knots and the rooftops of houses were appearing below us through the clouds, looking mighty close. As we began to accelerate and climb, I sighed a big sigh of relief and thanked God for his protection. I made the decision to proceed to Denver, our home base, and landed safely. God had spared me once again.

5

American Dream

"But whoso looketh into the perfect law of liberty, and continueth therein . . . this man shall be blessed in his deed"—James 1:25

I'm a country boy, and I was never content living in town, so around 1970 we bought a ten-acre plot of land just south of Brighton, Colorado, where we built our first home and played hobby farm. We raised some chickens, rabbits, geese, and beef cattle for our food supply, and, of course, we had to have a couple of horses to ride as well. We also got into gardening, and Juanita learned about canning and did a pretty good job of keeping our shelves supplied with home canned foods. Gary at age eight, Cindy at seven, and the tail-end kid and redheaded tiger Sharon at four loved country living and learned to enjoy the amenities it provided. They also learned how to work and take on responsibilities. It was a healthy and profitable character-building time for our family.

It was here that we transitioned to the independent Baptist church. The distance and time that it took to attend the Evangelical Free Church in Aurora caused us to look for a church a little closer to home. We found Elmwood Baptist Church, an independent Baptist church about ten minutes away and decided to see what it was like. The Bible was clearly preached, the doctrine was correct, and the Lord quickly made it clear to us that we were home as far as our church affiliation was concerned. We have stayed in independent Baptist churches and circles wherever we have moved since that time.

A few years later our pastor at Elmwood Baptist Church, Wilmer K. (Bill) Jones, suggested that I should take some voice lessons. He knew the voice teacher at Denver Baptist Bible College, Professor Don Scovill, and recommended I call him. When I called and asked about the possibility of getting voice lessons from him, Professor Scovill replied, "I don't normally give private lessons," he said, "But in talking to you, I believe you have something to offer and I would like to meet you."

I arranged to stop by the college on my way to the airport to fly a trip, and from that time on, for the next year, I would meet Don Scovill at the college, either on my way out on a trip or coming home. We became close friends. He was an immense help to me, later helping me cut a record, which is listened to in homes all across the country and even on a radio station in Africa. Many years later I was able to transfer the recording to a compact disc.

Don Scovill, second from left, and students

Our spiritual journey up to this point had been long and hard, and spiritual growth had come ever so slowly, because we had had very little mentoring or good Bible preaching and teaching. God so tenderly, patiently, and miraculously led us in our lives to where He wanted us to be, both spiritually and physically.

God knew what he was doing when he moved us to Brighton, Colorado, and Elmwood Baptist Church to be under the ministry of Pastor

Jones. It was there that we really began to learn how to live the Christian life. It was there that we learned to tithe, learned something about biblical standards, learned how to love and care for others in ways that we never had before, and learned how to share the gospel with others. We learned that obedience brings blessing and disobedience brings conflict. We learned we were grieving the Holy Spirit of God by frequenting movie theaters and wasting precious time in front of the TV, eating our meals off TV trays. These things are rarely preached against today, but they were desperately needed messages for our lives and home.

Ridding our home of the TV set was undoubtedly one of the most important decisions we ever made for our family. Through the preaching I became convicted about the time we were spending in front of the TV. One evening I arrived home from a Frontier flight around 10 p.m. and found my family watching TV. Gary was only eight years old, and I felt the children should have been in bed by that time. I shut the TV off and we tucked the children into their beds, and then Juanita and I had a conversation over the TV issue. I requested that she limit the children's time watching TV and to please have the children in bed a little earlier. Being the sweet compliant wife that she always has been, she apologized and agreed with my concerns and new convictions. About two weeks later, however, upon my arrival home late one evening I found the family watching TV again. We put the children to bed, and we decided to rid our home of the TV to avoid the temptation in obedience to the Word of God. My family was not too happy with me for a while, but after we showed the children how to enjoy the outdoors and find things to do, they soon adjusted and learned to enjoy the wonders of God's creation. They developed their imaginations and a love of the outdoors and never missed TV again. With no TV, we enjoyed the ten acres God had blessed us with even more, and family time around the Word of God became much more consistent.

While we were at Elmwood Baptist, Pastor Jones led the congregation to start a Christian school and encouraged his people to get out of the public school and secular indoctrination system, which we understood and did. We had a big part in establishing the Christian school, and moving our children from the public school system to the Christian school was another Holy Spirit-led and God-blessed decision for our family.

Our hobby farm adventure brought about opportunities for many exciting things. We decided to build a large detached garage and shop where I could pursue projects of interest. I found an ad in the paper for a Piper PA-12 aircraft and a Ford backhoe for sale, which I ended up buying for a total of 5000 dollars. The PA-12 was intact but needed considerable work, so my brother Bill and I tackled it in my new shop, and within a few months we had the PA-12 flyable and back in the air. We then were able to develop a short, barely sufficient air strip on our property, which afforded us many hours of enjoyment as a family and opportunities to give rides to others.

As much as we enjoyed our little hobby farm, it was not too many years before I began to search for a larger acreage and a place to build a larger home for our growing family. God had blessed us with three natural born children, but now God was leading us to adopt two children of Mexican descent. Lisa, age nine, and Gerald, age six, were brother and sister and were living in a foster home. We had known their foster mother as a teenager when we were in Omaha, Nebraska, and attending the Evangelical Free Church. She had grown up, married, and moved to Brighton, Colorado. Knowing that we were living in the Brighton area, she contacted us, and we soon became acquainted with Lisa and Gerald. They were close in age to our children and began to spend much time with us. The Lord began to speak to my heart about adopting these children who needed a permanent home and family. After much thought and prayer, I approached Juanita and asked her what she thought about the possibility.

"If you believe that God is leading us to do that, then we need to pursue it and see what the Lord does." she responded.

We carefully informed our children that we were praying about adopting Lisa and Gerald and asked for their thoughts. All three were excited about the possibility and thought we should move forward. We told them that if Lisa and Gerald became part of the family, they would have to move over and share all that they had, including their parents. They seemed to understand and were agreeable and enthusiastic, so we made an application. Six months later the adoption was finalized, and Lisa and Gerald became part of the Warinner family. We never once heard our original three complain or suggest that they wished that we had not adopted Lisa and Gerald. They received them with hearts of love, which endures to this day.

My dear wife Juanita has always been a loving, giving, submissive wife, willing to follow my lead, whatever that entailed. When we were still dating, she told me, "Where thou goest, I will go," and she obviously meant it, because she has stayed by my side through thick and thin, for 63 years, through all of life's many and varied adventures. I believe she has been as close to a Proverbs 31 lady as any woman could be, and I thank God for her! We could never have done all that the Lord has allowed us to do were it not for her love and faithfulness.

At the beginning we had little understanding about what we were gettin into with Lisa and Gerald, but God knew, and his grace is always sufficient. There were huge adjustments for all of us, but I think especially for Juanita. Gerald had special needs that we neither understood nor were trained to handle. Lisa had been abused and had never learned to trust anyone, so we had our work cut out for us in ways we could never have known. *But God!* God knew all that our family was facing, and by his love, mercy, and enabling grace we muddled through. All of our children have trusted Christ as their personal Savior; they love the Lord; they love one another; and all are faithful, serving in their respective Bible-preaching churches. To God be the glory!

My search for more acreage led us to purchase 160 acres four miles southeast of Hudson, Colorado. We picked a spot along the road to build our house, chose a house plan that we liked out of a magazine, and went to work on our great American dream. Dick Krentz, a builder and fellow member of Elmwood Baptist, offered to help us build our new home. We put our hobby farm up for sale, and it quickly sold.

Dick and I went to work on the new construction. We had the basement dug and the foundation and concrete block basement walls laid, when we had to close on our house and move. During the construction phase and before we found a place to hang our hats, we borrowed a pickup camper, and Juanita and I lived on site. Our children stayed with friends from church. Juanita and I took baths in a stock tank, and I built a toilet by stacking concrete blocks on three sides for privacy with a large block for the toilet seat. It was functional, but not the most comfortable. During this time, we leased the land to a local farmer, since we had neither the knowhow nor the equipment to work the land. One day when

Juanita was sitting on that concrete block toilet, our farmer came driving by with his tractor. We don't think he was aware of her being there, but needless to say, it was one of life's many embarrassing moments. Soon after that we were able to move into a little farmhouse that we rented just a quarter mile from the new place. The seven of us were stuffed into this little place, but we managed, and it was convenient during the time of the building project.

The new house didn't look that big to me, but Dick said as we began to dig the basement, "This is going to be a big house." As the project progressed and we started buying more and more materials, the reality of its size began to sink in. The house would be 4500 square feet, with five bedrooms, three on the main floor and two down, and a fully finished, walkout basement. We lived in the basement while we finished the main level, so we had a full kitchen there, a fireplace, and a large recreation room.

Our new home turned out to be a beautiful place. Life was wonderful on the farm, and it was such a great training ground for our children. Some of their fondest memories go back to that farm. We raised a garden, just as we had before, which kept our children busy weeding and Juanita busy canning. We also made it look like a real farm with our chickens, ducks, geese, a couple head of beef cattle, and a horse to ride.

Our children's friends loved to visit and ride the horse or mini bike, always having a great time. We planned to spend the rest of our days there, enjoying what was, to us, our great American dream.

Juanita and I had determined and felt led by the Lord that there ought to be consistency in the way we raised our children between the home, the church, and the school. We also felt the Lord would have us to exercise loving authority over their choice of friends and the atmosphere in which they spent time together as much as possible. God greatly blessed that philosophy.

We had sold the Piper PA-12 and went into partnership on a Cessna-172 with Max Witt, a friend of ours from Montview Evangelical Free Church, where we first attended church upon our move to the Denver area. We had the 172 for two or three years and then sold it also. Now without an airplane and desiring to teach Gary to fly, I found and purchased a Piper Super Cub PA-18 that one of our Frontier captains had for sale. Now we needed a hangar to store it in, so we built a Morton pole building large enough to store the Super Cub and other equipment and keep a little livestock. We also developed a half-mile runway that we flew from and where I taught Gary to fly, soloing him at age 16 and helping him get his private pilot license at age 17. To that point he had followed in his father's footsteps.

Cessna-172

Our children were really becoming very trustworthy and dependable, so one day Juanita and I went to Northglenn Mall, a shopping mall north of Denver, to do some shopping, and we left the children, now ages 12 through 16 at home. As we were driving up the road on our return home, we spotted Gary doing loops in the Super Cub. I almost had a heart attack! I had taught him how, but had *not* given him permission to perform that maneuver by himself! He survived, but after his landing, we had a little father to son conversation. Privately, I knew that I had done a lot more than that at his age and experience, but now I was talking to *my son* and from a depth of understanding that I had not possessed back then!

The farm was a real haven, and we sought to use it to be a blessing. We invited people over from church almost every Sunday and many from church and the Christian school in Longmont, where our children were enrolled, for special occasions such as Easter weekend and Thanksgiving. One Thanksgiving about 40 people came over. We gave airplane rides to most everyone, charging them a penny a pound to help cover the cost of fuel. It was a fun and blessed day.

Piper Super Cub PA-18

In 1978 we bought a new Pontiac station wagon and Gary, now 16, with his driver's license was able to drive to school. The trip to Longmont was 40 miles one way. Juanita and I had been driving the kids to and from school, many days making two trips and sometimes three for sports and so on. So, with a dependable car and a son with a driver's license, Gary became the driver for the school run and also picked up a couple of other kids along the way. It was a huge responsibility for a 16 year old. He proved himself, putting about 50,000 miles on that new car in the first year with no accidents or traffic tickets.

6
Changes

"A man's heart deviseth his way: but the Lord directeth his steps."
—*Proverbs 16:9*

The year 1978 was in many ways an exciting year for me. I had continued flying the Convair-580, and that year I upgraded to captain on the Boeing 737–200, a versatile and capable jet with seating for 115, which is still in service in some parts of the world today.

My copilot and me by the Boeing 737–200

However, 1978 also brought about sad times. That summer our family was on vacation in the Brainerd/Nisswa, Minnesota, area when the owner of the campground and resort where we were staying told me to contact my sister-in-law, Bill's wife Nancy. We reached her by telephone and learned that Bill had been killed in an aircraft accident while on a layover in Kalispell, Montana. Bill had been hired as a pilot with Frontier around 1964, had worked his way up the ladder, and was now flying copilot on the Boeing-737. He had made friends with an artist in the Kalispell area whom he was taking for a ride in a rented Piper Super Cub, looking for bear. He flew over the artist's home and dropped a note, but, being in mountainous terrain, apparently got into a down draft and was unable to recover. He entered the trees and impacted the ground inverted, killing both pilot and passenger instantly. Nancy had been trying to find us for several days, contacting the state patrol and anyone else she could think of, and finally catching up to us the day before the funeral. Bill left a wife and five children behind, the youngest only seven years of age.

Shocked, we quickly devised a plan for the children to stay with Juanita's parents while Juanita and I went to the funeral. We immediately packed, folded up our popup camping trailer, and headed for Minneapolis, where Juanita's parents lived, and then caught the next Frontier flight to Denver. Everything worked out, and we made the funeral on time. Funerals can be difficult occasions, especially when it involves family whose soul's salvation is unsure. Bill and I had been quite close and had done many things together since childhood: hunting, rebuilding aircraft, and building projects in our own homes. It was a tough period of adjustment being without Bill.

Bob, Larry, and Bill

We had realized our great American dream with a beautiful home on 160 acres, an airplane and hangar, a new car and five children faithfully in church and in a Christian school. We were growing in the Lord, and life couldn't have been much better, but little did we know that God was preparing our hearts for even bigger things ahead.

Pastor Bill Jones resigned his pastorate at Elmwood Baptist and moved to Illinois, and we eventually felt led by the Lord to transfer our membership to Tri-Town Baptist Church in Frederick, where Pastor Bob Roark was the pastor. God used Pastor Roark in a wonderful way, in my life especially. It was under his ministry that God convicted me about getting up early, about 5:00 a.m., to spend time in the word and pray. As a result, I grew in the Lord, and our family reaped the benefits of that growth. We began to be even more faithful with family devotions, and I started teaching a Sunday school class and preached now and then in nursing home services in Longmont. We became faithful in the church calling program and served in any way the Lord led, including having a big part in the new church building construction.

I had purchased an old International two-ton truck with a dump bed and a new Massy Ferguson diesel tractor with a frontend loader for the farm. I would load the tractor on the truck and haul it to the church project, then use the truck to pick up rock and fill dirt that was needed and move it around with the tractor, saving the church many hundreds of dollars.

About this time the inevitable changes began to take place. Gary graduated from high school and went off to Pillsbury Baptist Bible College in Owatonna, Minnesota, which left Cindy to do the driving to school, 40 miles one way. I soon became very uncomfortable with that arrangement and decided that either the farm would have to go, or we would have to pull the girls out of the Christian school. After much prayer, we decided to sell the farm, believing that keeping our children in the Christian school was more important for the long-term welfare of our family.

In the fall of 1979 we sold our beautiful home and property, where we had thought we would spend the rest of our lives, and moved to a home that we had purchased in Longmont where the girls would have only a short way to travel to school. We missed the farm, but we were also certain we were where we needed to be for the time.

In the process of selling the farm, we also sold the Piper Super Cub PA-18 to a missionary in the Philippines and purchased a Beech Debonair B-33, basing it at the Longmont airport.

At that time, I began to consider a new direction for our family in preparation for the days when my airline flying days would be history. Since Juanita and I are both from Minnesota, and since we love the water and boating, I decided to look for a small summer resort in northern Minnesota where we could spend our summers, enjoy family fun, and have a business write-off while doing it. I prayed about this move and became convinced in my heart that it was something the Lord would have us do. Little did I know what God really had in store for us.

The resort business in northern Minnesota is seasonal for the most part, running from Memorial Day to Labor Day, and my idea was to return to Longmont, Colorado, after Labor Day to put the kids back into school so that I would not have to commute during the winter months.

Juanita was somewhat resistant to the resort idea because it meant a lot of work! But, being the sweet, submissive wife that she always has been, we flew the Debonair on several trips to Minnesota, looking for a small family resort and finally settling on Riverside Resort Motel in Park Rapids, Minnesota. God knows what He is doing, even when we have no idea! Little did we know that through this move God was about to change our lives forever—and for the best.

Riverside Resort in Park Rapids, Minnesota

Riverside Resort had seven motel, housekeeping-type cabins, separated by carports; one separate cabin; and a small unit above the two-car garage, for a total of nine rentable units. The home was about 2500 square feet with a full basement, and the resort office was on the north end, off the living room area. We were now in the resort business, and I was doing what I once said I would never do, believing anyone who did it would have to be a little crazy. I would drive to Fargo, North Dakota, and commute on Frontier Airlines to Denver to fly my schedule, and then reverse the process, leaving Juanita and the kids to run the resort.

We had a lot to learn about the tourism industry and commuting, as well as many adjustments to make. In spite of this, the first summer went pretty well, and for the most part we all liked our new environment. It was a lot of work, but the rewards were worth it. We had many opportunities to be a witness for Christ and share the gospel, which was a rich experience in itself.

Gerald, Lisa, Gary, Juanita, Bob, Sharon, and Cindy

One night when I was on my commute home to Park Rapids, one of the most interesting witnessing events of my life took place. A year earlier I had taken my family on Frontier Airlines passes to visit my mother and sisters in Oregon. The flight was full, and available seating would not allow for all of us to sit together. I began to witness to the man sitting next to me and had a good time sharing the gospel with him until he deplaned in Boise, Idaho. It was now one year later, and as I was on my way home we landed in Rapid City, South Dakota, waiting to continue to Fargo, North Dakota, where I would pick up my car and continue my journey home. The flight was full out of Denver as usual, and I was on the jump seat in the cockpit. The flight pretty well emptied out in Rapid City, and my routine was to go back in the cabin, grab a row of seats, prepare a little nest, and take a nap en route to Fargo. While I was building my nest, one of the male passengers walked past me in the aisle a couple of times before he stopped next to me, pointed a finger, and loudly said, "Now I know who you are!"

I was a little startled, and he proceeded to remind me of my trip to Oregon a year earlier. He shared with me that he had been seated in the row in front of me and had been eavesdropping on my conversation as I shared the gospel with the man on the way to Boise. He asked if he could sit with me and talk. Of course, I invited him to do so, and I had the privilege of sharing the gospel with him all the way to Fargo. The seed was planted that night, and though to my knowledge he did not trust Christ at that time, God promises his word will not return unto him void but will accomplish that which he pleases.

We became very active in First Baptist Church in Park Rapids, where Warren Klenk was the pastor and Christian school administrator. By this time Lisa, Gary, and Cindy had graduated from high school and were off to Bible College, leaving Sharon and Gerald at home. Come Labor Day, it was time to close the resort and go back to Longmont for school, but upon my return from a flight with Frontier, I discovered that Sharon did not want to return to Longmont for school. She wanted to stay in Park Rapids and attend school at First Baptist instead. What's more, she had talked her mother into it! Juanita was in favor of staying in Park Rapids permanently, and after much discussion and prayer, I succumbed to the desires of my persuasive girls. But now I was commuting full time, and I knew I had gone crazy. Our home in Longmont sold fairly quickly, and we made our move to Park Rapids. This move was not part of my original plan, but God knew all along! Commuting in the winter was challenging at times, but the family was happy in Park Rapids.

I began my commute by flying our Beech Debonair from Park Rapids to Fargo, then jumping on a Frontier flight to Denver. One night on my return trip to Park Rapids, I ran into cloudy conditions with ceiling and visibility below weather minimums for a landing approach. I knew the area well, but it was late at night, and I had get-home-itis. Arriving at Park Rapids, I shot the approach to runway 31. When I saw the runway, I felt I did not have enough runway length left to make the landing, so I pulled up and went around for another approach. Juanita was waiting to pick me up and saw my red rotating beacon as I disappeared back into the clouds.

Beech Debonair

There was a potato chip factory about a half mile off the approach end of runway 31 that was well lit up at night, and on my second approach, for some reason I went unconscious for a few seconds or so, and when I regained consciousness, I was on a heading of 270 degrees, and about 100 feet over the factory. I spotted the runway out the right side of my windshield and made a steep right turn; I managed to get lined up with the runway and landed. I parked, got out, and kissed the ground, thanking the Lord for a safe landing, and vowed never to commute with the airplane again. From then on, I drove the two hours each way. God was not through with me yet! He preserved my life that night, enabling me to continue to serve Him all these years. *Glory to God!*

In the fall of 1983 a couple by the name of Dennis and Lee Deneau came to town presenting a ministry they called Bearing Precious Seed, a Scripture printing and distribution ministry that had started in Ohio ten years earlier. They pulled into Riverside Resort with a popup trailer, and we put them in a cabin free of charge. Thus began a lifelong influence and friendship that would once again forever change the course of our lives. Our church became very involved in the Bearing Precious Seed ministry in the months following their presentation, and after returning from a trip in April of 1984, I found Dennis Deneau in our resort office on the phone with missionary Bob Adams of Wings Bearing Precious Seed. As I walked in, Dennis said, "Let me put you on the phone with Bob Warinner . . ." Bob Adams was organizing a meeting with pilots in Memphis, Tennessee, within the next couple of weeks, and wanted me to attend. Bob Adams was trying to build a team of pilots that would be interested in joining him in his ministry of Scripture distribution throughout Mexico and Central America. I told him I would try to make the meeting, and he said that he could pick me up in Memphis, since my schedule would allow me to arrive in Memphis the night before his meeting.

Missionary Bob Adams and wife Mary

After flying my three-day trip and arriving back in Denver, all I wanted was to go home, so I called Bob Adams and informed him that I would not make it to his meeting. He nearly began to cry. Apparently, I was the only pilot who was planning to attend. He asked if there was any way that I could meet him and talk with him. I finally agreed and caught the next flight out to Memphis.

Bob Adams was a great blessing, and we had a wonderful time together. One other pilot did show up: Bill Horner, a former fighter pilot in the Vietnam War who had flown several mission trips with Bob Adams. After a good time of discussion together as Bob Adams shared the need and his vision to meet that need, I boarded a flight for Fargo to pick up my car and drive home, with many thoughts in my mind. I had been thinking about and praying for God's leading and direction for many years. My earlier calling to missions had not been forgotten, and here God was presenting me with an opportunity to serve him with my background in aviation.

In June of 1984 First Baptist Church held its first Bearing Precious Seed conference. We closed the resort to the public and housed most of our out-of-town attendees there. Among many others who attended was Dr. Don Frazer, founder of the Bearing Precious Seed ministry. One night as Dr. Frazer retired to his cabin sometime after midnight, he asked me to knock at his door and wake him at 6 a.m., which I agreed to do. The next morning, I knocked on his door, and Dr. Frazer asked me to come in and talk with him. He was fully dressed and seemed ready for our interview. Upon entering, he motioned for me to sit.

"Do you see anything strange about that curtain over there on the window?" he asked. I looked at the curtain. I had no idea what he was thinking about.

"No, I don't," I said. The curtain was hanging smartly on its rod and had the print of a flying eagle on it, just like it always had.

"Don't you see?" he pointed. "The eagle on the curtain has only one wing, and that's the problem with the Bearing Precious Seed ministry. It has only one wing. Brother Bob, would you be that other wing?"

I knew now what he meant: Bob Adams was the lone wing in the transporting of Scriptures to Mexico and Central America, and he needed help. Dr. Frazer was asking if I would use my abilities and my experience for the Lord and be that other wing.

Dennis Deneau on left and Dr. Don Frazer

7

Wings As Eagles Mission Air Service

"But they that wait upon the Lord shall renew their strength; they shall mount up with wings as eagles...... "—Isaiah 40:31

I was still flying for Frontier Airlines while running the resort with two children still at home. Now we believed the Lord was calling us to start a ministry to help provide Scriptures to missionaries on the field. I had told Dr. Frazer I would pray about it. I did pray and seek the Lord's leading, also consulting with my wife and family. In July of 1984 God laid it upon our hearts to start the ministry we call Wings As Eagles Mission Air Service, deriving the name from Isaiah 40:31.

We didn't feel led to join forces with Bob Adams' ministry at that time, but instead to remain where we were in Park Rapids. We began the ministry of Wings As Eagles on our own, working in concert with Bob Adams and the Bearing Precious Seed ministry. It would take us some months to lay the foundations for the new ministry. We visited churches to present the ministry and raise support. There were also necessary changes in our lifestyle that we needed to make that would give us the freedom to devote ourselves to the ministry.

When I counseled with Dr. Frazer about launching the Wings ministry, he gave me advice and instructions that he called tools and then told me to go do it. I had preached only a little in nursing homes, taught a little in Sunday school, and served in the calling and visitation ministries of the church. I felt so incapable and unprepared for such a task, but Philippians 4:13 assured me that *"I can do all things through Christ which strengtheneth me."* God did give me the enabling grace that I needed.

Another man at that first Bearing Precious Seed conference that year was missionary Carlos Demarest, who had pastored for many years and at that time was heading up the Bearing Precious Seed ministry in El Paso, Texas, under the arm of First Baptist Church of Milford, Ohio, under Pastor Charles Keen. Carlos Demarest operated short-term mission trips with a large bus into Mexico, filling the bus with both people and Scriptures to distribute to villagers.

Carlos Demarest's bus

Juanita and I were privileged to go on several mission trips into Mexico with Carlos on his bus before the Wings ministry got fully established. Those trips were a blessing and encouragement to us, and we longed for the time when the Wings ministry would function in a similar way.

On one such trip we went to a village named Ejido Constitución. We were told that a couple of years earlier when Carlos had stopped there with a group, a middle-aged lady who lived there asked what brought them to town. When Carlos said that they were going to a village up the road to start a gospel preaching church. She replied, "We need a church here! Why don't you start a church here?" Carlos took that invitation as from the Lord, and a missionary did start a church there, which by the time we visited was being led by a national pastor and was doing well. What a great blessing it was to meet that dear Mexican lady who had been instrumental in the church start up in her village and to see the faithfulness of the church members in that small village.

Juanita and Mexican lady who asked Carlos Demarest to start a church in her village

I learned a song from an evangelist entitled *He Paid a Debt*, and I taught it to Carlos. He loved that song, and he sang it wherever he went with a group—in restaurants, airports, anywhere. One time Carlos met Juanita and me at the terminal as we arrived in El Paso, and as we deplaned, he started singing that song. Of course, we all chimed in. When we finished, the ticket agents and others clapped enthusiastically and thanked us. That type of response was far more common than not.

He Paid a Debt
He paid a debt He did not owe; I owed a debt I could not pay;
I needed someone to wash my sins away.
And now I sing a brand new song,
"Amazing Grace" the whole day long!
Christ Jesus paid a debt that I could never pay.

He paid that debt at Calvary; He cleansed my soul and set me free;
I'm glad that Jesus did all my sins erase.
I now can sing a brand new song,
"Amazing Grace" the whole day long!
Christ Jesus paid a debt that I could never pay.

> One day He's coming back for me to live with Him eternally;
> Won't it be glory to see Him on that day!
> I then will sing a brand new song,
> "Amazing Grace" the whole day long!
> Christ Jesus paid a debt that I could never pay.

Carlos Demarest has now gone home to be with the Lord, but at that time he was an avid and faithful witness for the Lord. He was another man who had a great influence on both our lives and our ministry. Few people came into contact with Carlos without being touched with the gospel in some way.

In the fall of 1984, after officially establishing the Wings ministry and with much fear and trepidation, I began to contact pastors sharing that the Lord had laid on my heart to start the ministry of Wings As Eagles. Its purpose would be to take the Scriptures printed by the Bearing Precious Seed ministries distributing them to missionaries in Canada, Mexico, Central America, and the Caribbean, getting pastors to go along and participate in that effort.

As I made those phone calls, most pastors were kind, but some questioned why they should fly with me and not take the airlines. I would explain that they would be supporting God's work instead of the world and its economy. They would be flying with pilots who were prayed up instead of pilots who were drunk up. We wouldn't lose their luggage, and, very importantly, we could go places that the airlines could not go. I must admit that at times their questioning opposition was discouraging, but God had given me a burden and would not let me quit.

Pastor Joe Minnerup of White Oak Baptist Church, a little country church about 20 miles east of Park Rapids, graciously scheduled a meeting with us and allowed us to present our new ministry in January of 1985. That meeting with was our beginning, and his church took us on for 15 dollars per month. What encouragement that was to us!

Several years later, Pastor Minnerup would resign his ministry at White Oak Baptist, and I would lose contact with him for about 20 years. We also eventually lost our support from that church. Then, years later, when he heard that Juanita had had surgery for breast cancer, he contacted us to find out how she was doing. By then he was pastoring Berean Baptist Church in Minot, North Dakota, and invited us, if we were ever out that way, to please stop in and present the Wings ministry to his church. About two months later when we were in the area, we did have a meeting in his church. In my presentation, I jokingly said that I was there to get that 15 dollars a month support back and that I wanted it retroactive! Instead Pastor Minnerup recommended to the church that they support us at 100 dollars per month ongoing. Our friendship and their support continue to this day. What a God we serve! That original 15 dollars in 1985 gave us such hope and confidence. It was God telling us to keep on keeping on, and we did.

8

Wings Aloft

"Mine eye affecteth mine heart……."—*Lamentations 3:51*

In April of 1985 Missionary Bob Adams of Wings Bearing Precious Seed invited me to take our first Wings As Eagles mission trip with him to Veracruz, Mexico, to visit and work with missionary Don Rogers and his family for a few days. I invited our pastor, Pastor Warren Klenk, and our son Gary to go along. The three of us took off from ParkRapids on the appointed day and headed for Halls, Tennessee. Upon our approaching Halls, the weather was low overcast, and we were flying on top of the overcast. Halls airport is small and did not have an approach facility that would enable us to shoot an approach and land in the poor weather, so we prayed, asking the Lord to open a hole in the clouds so that we could descend. As our navigation equipment indicated we were just about over the airport, a hole in the clouds opened up. We descended through the hole and safely landed. Bob Adams, who was waiting for us, had also been asking the Lord to part the clouds.

Together we thanked God for his goodness and began to plan our departure for Mexico the next morning. Bill Horner, who had been working with Bob Adams and had used his aircraft on several mission trips, would be flying in with his Cessna-206 a little later that evening, and we planned to take his plane into Mexico. After his arrival we removed three seats and loaded his airplane with 450 pounds of Scriptures and decided that, due to our load, Gary and Bob Adams would have to stay back, while Pastor Klenk and I accompanied Bill to Veracruz. I hated to leave them, but we didn't have much choice due to our gross weight limitations in the 206.

The next foggy morning before daylight, with Bill Horner at the controls, me in the right seat, and Pastor Klenk in the remaining seat in the back, Bill completed the engine runup and applied full power for takeoff. After liftoff we broke out above the fog to beautiful clear skies, with the sun beginning to rise, and everything running smoothly. We were on our way to Veracruz! My heart was thrilled to be launching our first official Wings As Eagles mission trip!

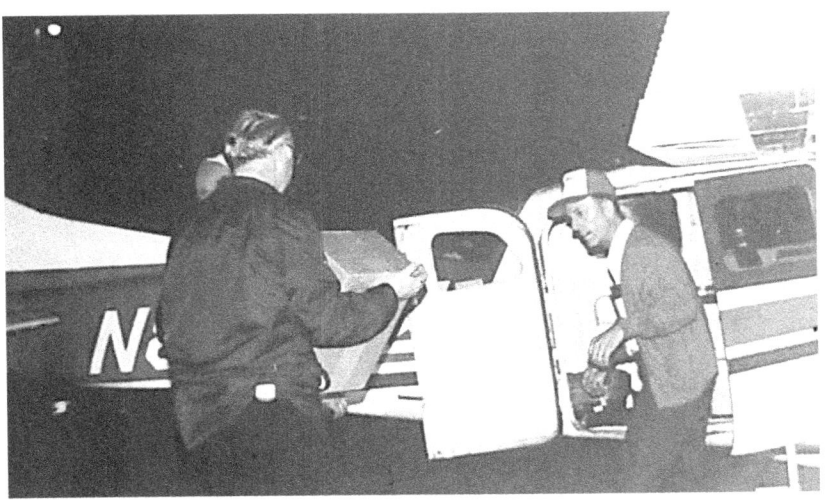

Pastor Klenk and Bill Horner loading aircraft with Scriptures

We made a couple of fuel stops and then cleared Mexican customs in Matamoros. Knowing that I would soon be handling the customs process myself, I was careful to pay close attention to all that Bill Horner did.
When we arrived in Veracruz, missionary Don Rogers was at the airport to meet us and take us to his home, where we had the opportunity to get acquainted with his dear family. We prepared for our departure for a mission work he was involved with several hours' drive northwest of Veracruz. The drivers in Mexico are extremely careless, making three lanes out of a two-lane road, passing on curves, and breaking just about every common sense driving rule people of our culture can imagine. It is a wonder that anyone survives! But we arrived without incident at a little village where an hour and a half hike up the mountain awaited us.

In the village at the foot of the mountain, we met the national pastor. Over the course of our conversation, we discovered that he had been praying about the need for Bibles but had no idea where or how he could obtain them. Although his prayer was unknown to us before that day, we had transported the Scriptures to that remote village and were the answer to his prayer, fulfilling his request on the spot!

We all rejoiced and gave glory to God. In Isaiah 65:24 God's Word says, *"And it shall come to pass, that before they call, I will answer; and while they are yet speaking, I will hear."* Here was an answered prayer that I was able to have a part in, and God greatly increased my faith through it all.

The trek up the mountain was led by a 74-year-old national who put those of us from the United States to shame with his stamina. Don Rogers had, of course, been to this Totonac Indian village several times before, and the natives were delighted to see him again. We were all greeted warmly and kindly. We were blessed to see that the spirit of the Lord Jesus Christ shines through in the lives of those who know him. We experienced a shared connection, even though we do not share a common language.

Pastor Klenk, Don Rogers, and our guide

That night Don preached, with many of the villagers showing up for the service. The natives generously shared their meager food supplies with us, and after a time of fellowship we settled in for the night. I had the pleasure of sleeping on a 2x12 board elevated between two concrete blocks, which was a first for me, and I did manage to get some much-needed sleep. The next morning, starting about 3:30, the roosters in the village began to crow, making sleep more difficult from that time on. About 6:00 a.m. it was rise-and-shine time. Our hosts served us a breakfast of eggs, black beans, and corn tortillas.

Totonac ladies

Later that morning we headed back down the mountain, which was much easier and much faster than the trek up. Arriving in the village where we had left the car, we loaded up and headed for Veracruz. It was foggy, and visibility was very poor. All of a sudden, we came up behind a vehicle stopped in our lane. Don swerved around it, and by God's grace there were no oncoming vehicles in the opposite lane! We all sighed with relief and thanked the dear Lord for his protection. That incident was a clear reminder that the devil will try to destroy those who try to serve the Lord. Here was a moment, one among many which I have had since, when my companions and I experienced God's hand of protection and saw how narrowly we escaped. *Glory to God!*

Don Rogers, wife, and three youngest children

Safely back in Veracruz, we spent the remainder of the day and night at the Rogers' home enjoying sweet fellowship. The next morning Don drove us to the airport for our flight back to Halls, Tennessee. It is quite a process to leave Mexico, just as it is to enter, and after about an hour of trotting from one office to another, filling out forms and paying various fees, we were finally fueled and ready to depart for McAllen, Texas, to clear customs back into the States. Bill Horner was doing the flying, and Pastor Klenk was in the right seat. Shortly after departure I began to feel sick, and it wasn't long before I felt so miserable that I thought I was going to die. Apparently, I had drunk some bad water somewhere, and it was taking its toll. Since we no longer had the load of Bibles, there was room for me to lie on the floor, which I gladly did. Upon arrival at McAllen, I made a mad rush for the men's room and found some much needed relief.

After clearing US customs, refueling, and filing a new flight plan to Halls, we launched once again. I was still not feeling my best by a long shot and, upon arriving at our next fuel stop, I repeated the dash to the facilities. By the time we made it to Halls, I felt somewhat better. Bob Adams got me some buttermilk, which I like, and sent me to bed to recoup before our trip back to Park Rapids the next day. I felt much better the next morning! Gary, Pastor Klenk, and I had a good trip home, rejoicing over all the things we had seen and done and how God was raising up a new ministry for his glory.

Pastor Klenk in lifechanging thought

Lamentations 3:51 says, *"Mine eye affecteth mine heart........"* Pastor Klenk was profoundly moved by this trip and all he had experienced and seen. God was doing a great work in his heart that was changing his life forever. Every message he preached for several weeks had to do with our mission trip. A short time later Pastor Klenk resigned as pastor and went to serve full time with the Bearing Precious Seed ministry and Pastor Keen in Milford, Ohio. He was there for about two years, and then he and his dear wife Joanne went to Mexico where they served the Lord as missionaries for about 23 years. Now in their 80s, they grieve that they have had to leave their ministry with their beloved Mexican people and go back to the States to be near family. Pastor Klenk and Joanne have been a great blessing and godly influence in our lives, for which we are so grateful.

9

Learning to Trust

". . . There is no man that hath left house, or parents, or brethren, or wife, or children, for the kingdom of God's sake, Who shall not receive manifold more in this present time, and in the world to come life everlasting."—Luke 18:29–30

Juanita and I continued to stay busy with the resort while I flew for Frontier and made calls to pastors, trying to get meetings to present our burden and the ministry the Lord had now firmly placed on our hearts. We tried to schedule meetings during the months of October through April when the resort was closed to the public. By this time, I was senior enough with Frontier so that I could bid schedules that gave me Sundays off and, in some cases, we could ride on a pass with Frontier to a scheduled meeting.

I had so much to learn about preaching; about how to present the ministry; and about how to talk with pastors, answer their questions, and rebut their skepticism. The pastors who gave us meetings were gracious and patient, even though I was like the notorious bull in a china shop. God blessed in wondrous and mighty ways, proving that He certainly does use *". . . the foolish things of the world to confound the wise; and . . . the weak things of the world to confound the things which are mighty"* I Corinthians 1:27. We kept doing what God had called us to do, managing to convince a few pastors to take mission trips with us on a love-gift basis while I was flying for the airline. I found out quickly that love gifts were not going to cover costs, so we began to ask our passengers to share in the direct costs if at all possible.

Frontier Airlines was experiencing some management issues, and in July of 1986 the company filed bankruptcy and ceased operation. Continental Airlines bought the airplanes and absorbed the pilots, offering severance packages to those who chose to leave or retire. I had received a communiqué from Continental to report to Houston, Texas, for training, but at that time, I really felt the Lord was telling me to leave the airline industry and go full time with Wings As Eagles. Therefore, I took the severance package, which amounted to a rather meager sum of money and airline passes on Continental for the next 20 years, plus accumulated retirement funds over my years of service, which would beforthcoming.

Juanita struggled a little with all of this, being deeply concerned that we might never get to see our children Gary and Lisa, who by now had each married and were still living in the Denver area. Juanita's faith may have been small at that time, but little did we know that God would take us back to Denver in future years in a way we never could have guessed!

Our more than adequate income now gone, we had to daily seek God's wisdom, provision, and clear direction. We were learning to trust God in ways that tested our faith a little sooner than planned. As always, God proved himself faithful. Proverbs 3:5–8 tells us to *"Trust in the LORD with all thine heart; and lean not unto thine own understanding. In all thy ways acknowledge him, and he shall direct thy paths. Be not wise in thine own eyes: fear the LORD, and depart from evil. It shall be health to thy navel, and marrow to thy bones."* These verses became very applicable to our experience, and they are now among my very favorite.

In the summer of 1986, shortly after I left Frontier Airlines, Francisco "Paco" Guerrero, a national missionary from Tampico, Mexico, visited our church in Park Rapids. He needed to get to a meeting he had scheduled at Prayer Baptist Church in Detroit, Michigan, so I offered to fly him there in our Beech Debonair. At that meeting the pastor took up an offering, and the Holy Spirit impressed upon my heart to give the money that I had reserved to purchase fuel for our return trip. I wrestled with that urge before the plate came by, but when the offering plate came to me, I obediently surrendered the 50-dollar bill. Since I didn't have a credit card, I wasn't sure what I would do about fuel for the trip home. About 30 minutes later the preacher announced that he felt led by God to give every missionary present a love gift of 100 dollars. God returned to me double what I had given just 30 minutes before! I could hardly believe it. Luke 6:38 says, *"Give, and it shall be given unto you; good measure, pressed down, and shaken together, and running over, shall men give into your bosom. For with the same measure that ye mete withal it shall be measured to you again."* God was teaching me so much, and I was reminded once again that obedience brings blessing, and disobedience brings conflict.

The meeting at Prayer Baptist Church was a great blessing in more ways than one. Pastor Story, one of the pastors I met, had a son Ron who had become a very successful businessman. Ron was also a private pilot who owned a Beech King Air B-90 aircraft. Ron took me out to see his aircraft, and flew it around the patch a couple of times. We made plans to use it on a mission trip together. Ron Story became a great blessing to the Wings ministry, as we used his aircraft on at least three mission trips to Mexico and Honduras. We saw many souls saved, thousands of Bibles and Scripture portions distributed. The hearts of several pastors were burdened in a greater way towards mission outreaches at home and abroad.

We closed the resort as usual after Labor Day in 1986 and left shortly thereafter for meetings that by God's grace I was able to schedule in Michigan. After paying the mortgage on the resort and taking care of other obligations, we left on our first real deputation trip in our, by now, very high mileage 1978 Pontiac station wagon. We had about 100 dollars in our pocket. Our first meeting was with Pastor Don Green at Parker Memorial Baptist Church in Lansing, Michigan. Pastor Green very graciously took care of us, but a small incident took place there that we will never forget. God moved upon the heart of a boy about eight or nine years old to approach me and hand me a giving envelope saying that he wanted me to have it for our ministry. Upon opening the envelope, I found it contained one nickel. That gift from that little boy brought tears to my eyes, and I don't think a million dollars would have touched my heart any more than that nickel did! I still tear up when I think of that little boy and his gift. God shows himself mighty in such wonderful and tender ways.

God proved his love and ability to care for us on the trip, and we returned with about 2000 dollars for personal and ministry expenses.

Learning to be a gracious receiver of gifts when you are used to being a giver is rather humbling to say the least. It was a new experience for me. Dr. Frazer used to tell me that I needed to learn to receive as graciously as I gave. It was a hard lesson for me to learn, I suppose because of something called pride, wicked pride!

In November of 1986 Juanita and I, Pastor Minnerup, Ron Story, and Dave Webster took a trip to Tampico, Mexico, to work with Paco Guerrero. We had met Dave Webster a couple of years earlier in Park Rapids when he flew some men in from Prince Albert, Saskatchewan, Canada, for our Bearing Precious Seed Conference. Pastor Minnerup, Juanita and I flew to Detroit in our Beach Debonair and joined Ron Story and Dave Webster there. The next morning, we took off and headed for Tampico in Ron's Beech-90 King Air.

Paco was there to meet us when we arrived at the Tampico airport. We stayed in his home and enjoyed the time of fellowship with his family. The next day we loaded up some Scriptures and headed for a river port where we could charter a boat and captain to take us to a village up river where Paco wanted to minister and perhaps start a church work. The ride up river was about thirty to forty-five minutes, and we were all in deep thought and prayer as we motored on our way. Upon arrival at the village we disembarked the boat and went to homes around the village, giving out John and Romans booklets and inviting people to a preaching service later that day. We were well-received, and the open-air service was reasonably well-attended, with several people trusting Christ as their Savior.

After a little visiting we walked back to the landing and found our boat captain patiently waiting for us. Before our departure, Paco took time to witness and share the gospel with him.

We all climbed aboard and proceeded back to Tampico. I was so moved by all I had just experienced that I began to weep uncontrollably. I believe God was enlarging my vision, giving me compassion for people who need the Lord, challenging me to help meet those needs, cleansing my heart and soul—and it was all overwhelming.

I can't really explain all that was going on in my heart, but God has a purpose for tears. I have found that as I have gotten older the tears flow much more easily and frequently, and my heart has become more easily touched with the cares and needs of others.

Our boat captain, Paco, and me

After an evening of fellowship with Paco and his family, we retired for a good night's rest. The next morning we departed along with Paco for a visit with Don Rogers and his family in Veracruz, about 250 miles down the coast. It was a precious time. We returned to Tampico for a final night, and then it was time to go home. The performance of the King Air—its load, speed, and altitude capabilities—was a great blessing. I thank God for Ron Story and his generosity and desire to use the aircraft God had blessed him with in reaching the lost. I believe God expects inventions and development of technology to be used for his glory, and I have learned that without the airplane, many parts of the world and many precious souls would never be physically reached with the gospel.

Juanita and me with King Air

10

Beyond Our Horizon

"For as many as are led by the Spirit of God........"
—Romans 8:14

In the spring of 1986 Juanita and I were blessed with the inheritance of a 1957 Chevrolet from Juanita's great aunt. Shortly afterwards, missionary George Anderson, Director of Missionary Training Institute of Bowie, Texas, was in our church in Park Rapids, Minnesota, staying at our resort. In talking with George, I became aware of the need of missionary Lewis Young, a former student who was now serving with his family in a very remote village in Papua New Guinea. Lewis Young's only means of getting supplies was through either Missionary Aviation Fellowship and their helicopter service or a seven-to-eight-hour trek through the jungles to the nearest airstrip.

When I asked what it would take to construct a runway at his village, George told me that if Lewis Young had two or three thousand dollars, he thought he could see it accomplished using the natives. Juanita and I prayed about it and decided to sell the '57 Chevy and give the resources, which came to 2500 dollars, to Lewis in Papua New Guinea to construct a runway. Lewis was able to get the native villagers to work on the project, which took a year of digging as much as 20 feet into the mountainside. He supplied the tools, picks, shovels, and wheelbarrows, which were brought in by helicopter, and he fed the workers rice and fish.

The following February we had a meeting in Superior, Wisconsin, at Twin Ports Baptist Church with Pastor Rick Scarberry, a congenial, uncomplaining man with a quick wit and keen sense of adventure. We also shared much in common in the Lord. He was a real doer. He told me about a former Bible college schoolmate who was a missionary in Papua

New Guinea and suggested a mission trip there. I was very interested and excited, especially because of my earlier involvement in Lewis Young's runway project in Papua New Guinea. Rick wondered if it might be possible to go visit his former schoolmate using my Continental Airlines space-available passes. Instead of buying prohibitively expensive tickets, he would travel on my pass privileges as my companion, as long as there was space available on our chosen flights. I told him we could do that, so we began to make plans to visit not only Papua New Guinea later that year, but also Sydney, Australia, where another former schoolmate of his was serving as a missionary.

God was blessing the Wings ministry, and on occasion when my schedule allowed I would accompany Dennis Deneau as he traveled to churches to present the Bearing Precious Seed ministry. Our time together was profitable, not only for the fellowship, but also for picking each other's brains about the ministry, opening doors for me to get acquainted with other pastors, and introducing them to the Wings As Eagles ministry. Early in the fall of 1988 I accompanied Dennis to a church in Clinton, North Carolina, where I shared the Wings ministry with Pastor Emmett Bartlett. A short time later Pastor Bartlett received a complimentary airline ticket to travel to visit Pensacola Christian College in Pensacola, Florida, as did a number of other pastors. He was placed in a hotel room with Pastor Doug Kalapp from Victory Baptist Church in Jerseyville, Illinois. Doug had been on a mission trip to Mexico a month or so earlier, where he was kicked in the leg by a horse. He was using crutches when Pastor Bartlett asked him what had happened, he explained the situation. Doug also shared his vision to establish an aviation ministry that would take pastors and other people on short-term mission trips. He was a student pilot and had soloed, but he had no experience, so it would be a long time before he would be ready to fly those types of trips.

"You need to contact Bob Warinner!" Pastor Bartlett told him. "He just visited our church; he has a ministry named Wings As Eagles; and he's doing just what you have a vision to do!"

Doug asked for my phone number, but he didn't have it available at that time. He said he would call and give it to him as soon as he was back home.

I have heard that before, he thought; but Pastor Bartlett kept his word, and he did contact him later and gave him my number.

Now that I was no longer flying the airline, when I was home, I got up early and went to the church to get the fire going in the church furnace to warm things up for the school kids. While there, I would go to the nursery and spend time with the Lord in prayer. One particular morning early in October of 1988, I asked the Lord if he would mind if I just sat in the rocking chair and talked with him. I usually knelt, but this morning I just needed to sit. The trip to Papua New Guinea and Australia was only weeks away. I didn't know how we could keep pace with the ministry and the direction it was going. I was crying out to the Lord about needing a godly man with a vision to join us in this ministry. We needed help. I finished praying and went home, where Juanita met me at the door.

"A preacher by the name of Doug Kalapp just called and wants to talk with you," she told me. "Here's his number."

I called him back and we had a long talk, discovering that our vision for an aviation ministry was pretty much identical. We discussed plans for me to fly to Jerseyville and take him and another pastor friend on a mission trip to Jimenez, Chihuahua, Mexico, to work with missionary Lanny Ashcraft for a few days. He was an active preacher, and I an active and experienced pilot. God was putting together a team! We would find out what God had in store in the months to come, but now it was time to get ready for the trip Down Under!

11

Over Mountain and Jungle

"... and ye shall be witnesses unto me ... unto the uttermost part of the earth."—Acts 1:8

On Tuesday, October 18, 1988, our amazing Papua New Guinea/Australia adventure began. Juanita drove me to the Minneapolis airport, where I met Pastor Rick Scarberry and boarded a Continental Boeing-727 on schedule for Denver. From there we would travel to California, then to Hawaii, Guam, and finally to Papua New Guinea. After almost two weeks in PNG, we would retrace our steps to Guam and Hawaii, and from there travel to Australia for eight days before heading home again to Minnesota.

Upon our arrival in Denver, we found that the flights on to San Francisco and Los Angeles were both overbooked, so we were sent to the Oakland gate and managed to get on that flight. Arriving in Oakland, we caught a shuttle van to the San Francisco airport with about an hour and a half to spare before our flight to Honolulu, Hawaii. We boarded our flight, a Continental DC-10 bound for Honolulu, arriving on schedule late that evening.

We stayed at the Airport Holiday Inn for 61 dollars per night and hit the sack just after midnight. Rick was so excited he could hardly sleep. The loads were looking good for the next day's flights to Guam and on to Papua New Guinea.

The next morning, we were up early, and Rick led us in a short devotional out of Isaiah 60:1–3. I was excited to see what the Lord was going to accomplish in our lives through this trip! Since our flight to Guam was not scheduled to leave until 1:30 p.m., we went for a walk and caught a bus to Pearl Harbor for a brief tour. After taking the bus back to the airport, we boarded our flight to Guam, were seated in business class, and departed on time. Our passes entitled me to fly in business class and Rick to travel coach, but since there was an available seat in business class, we were able to sit together there. He was awestruck by the whole experience. We were served Cornish game, steak with all the trimmings, and apple pie for dessert. We really felt like the King's children!

Pastor Scarberry in Hawaii

When we arrived in Guam, a beautiful, tropical island territory in the Western Pacific Ocean, we found that our flight to Papua New Guinea had been canceled until the following day, Friday morning. We had crossed the international date line, jumping ahead a day, so it was now Thursday. It was a warm, humid, clear day as we left the airport and took a taxi to Fujita Hotel on the beach.

As soon as we got settled, Rick wanted to go for a swim in the ocean, so off we went. The water was very warm and clear with a white sand beach. We checked with Continental about the flight to New Guinea and were told that it was now canceled for another day, until Saturday. We found the local restaurants in Guam were very expensive, so we ended up going to a Kentucky Fried Chicken.

Early the next morning Rick awakened and couldn't sleep. I turned the light on a short time later and he sat up in his bed. We began talking about our lives and work and things of the Lord until daylight. Rick decided to go to the beach, while I stayed back spending time with the Lord before joining him there. He had the room key in the pocket of his swim trunks and unfortunately lost it in the ocean. We went to the hotel desk and were promptly advised that there would be a $50 charge if we could not return the key. On our limited budget, we panicked and decided we had better go back out and see if we could find it, even though that would take a miracle of God.

We prayed over the missing key and decided that he would go look for it while I stayed back in the room to call John Lewis, pastor of nearby Harvest Baptist Church to schedule time for fellowship later that day, and to try to find a more reasonably priced place to stay. About an hour later I went out, and saw him on his way back with the key in hand! Praise God! He *does* hear and answer the prayers of his children! My faith was bolstered, and our hearts were assured that God's hand was in this trip and that he would get us to Papua New Guinea. Rick shared with me that as he retraced his steps, he saw the sun's reflection glinting off the key. In my mind, that is nothing short of a miracle! God is so good!

Leaving the key safely in the room, he went back outside to attempt to break open a coconut by dropping it from our second-floor room to the pavement below. After one try, he went down to pick it up. I thought I would step out and help him by having him throw the coconut back to me, and I would throw it down again. Stepping out, I let the door close behind me, and we were locked out of our room once again! A maid happened to be passing by and was kind enough to let us back in. We never did get the coconut open!

We rented a car and met Pastor Lewis for lunch and then drove to his church, which had about 250 members. Their Christian school had around 800 students enrolled and appeared to be a first-class work, which continues to this day. We were blessed and impressed with what God was doing there. Pastor Lewis graciously arranged for us to spend that night with three single military service men from the church in their home overlooking the airport, city, and beach area.

On Saturday, October 22, we departed Guam for Port Moresby, the capital of Papua New Guinea, arriving there four days after leaving Minnesota. We had checked a box of Bibles in Minneapolis, but they failed to arrive with us. We prayed that we would be able to recover them, but we never did. We could only trust that the Lord had a more needful destination for them than what we had planned.

Missionary Ken Jenkins was waiting to meet us in Port Moresby when we arrived and put us up in a nice, clean apartment in the lower level of their home. The Jenkins family lived on a fenced-in compound near the outskirts of the city. Their church was in the compound also. Rick and I were both asked to preach somewhere on Sunday, so after studying, I turned out my light excited about what the Lord was doing! So far I had found Ken Jenkins to be a tremendous guy. His short and stocky build reminded me a lot of my brother Larry.

The next morning Rick taught Sunday school at the compound church, a small wood frame building with a concrete floor, wooden benches, and a seating capacity of about 100. I went with Ken to teach Sunday school at a nearby work that was just six weeks old, sharing from John chapter 3, the New Birth Chapter, as I've heard it referred to. The people were friendly and seemed excited to have us there. They had been looking for spiritual help for many years, and there was a sweet, open spirit in the new church. It was a blessed time for me to be able to share God's word with such friendly and enthusiastic people. A couple of men who were also staying with the Jenkins family while conducting a survey trip for future ministry went to preach the morning service for the patients at the Gerehu Hospital in Port Moresby, a ministry headed by a national Christian man. The men's hearts were so blessed as four patients trusted Christ. They were, however, astounded by the unsanitary conditions at the hospital.

After regathering at the compound after church, we went out for Japanese food and relaxed for the afternoon. We all attended the compound church together for the evening service, again a precious time together in the Lord. The people expressed how much they needed our visit and that we were a great encouragement to them.

On Monday we were all excited to travel to Wau, where Rick's former classmate, Jim Blume, was located. Before we left, Mrs. Jenkins fixed us a breakfast of ham, eggs, biscuits, and gravy, and then Ken took us to the bank to exchange some dollars to kina, where we lost about 18%. At the Talair Airline ticket counter we each purchased one-way tickets to Wau for 69 kina, or about 57 US dollars.

We boarded a Twin Otter, a high-wing, twin-engine aircraft capable of carrying about 20 passengers, and were on our way. The mountainous terrain was awesome! We were cruising at 12,500 VFR, (Visual Flight Rules) single pilot operation. Wau, a town of several thousand, sits in a valley at 3500 feet with mountains all around. We landed on a steep grass strip with a seven-degree uphill gradient.

Twin Otter

Jim Blume and family were on deck to greet us in Wau, and his wife Mary had a nice lunch waiting at their home. Jim showed us around town and introduced us to the national pastor, Tania Tia.

Jim Blume, Pastor Tia and family, and Pastor Scarberry

The weather on our arrival was beautiful, partly cloudy, but about an hour later it began to rain, and it rained all night. It rains about fifteen to eighteen feet a year there. We enjoyed an evening meal and fellowship until bedtime.

The next morning Jim took us on a flying trip to three different villages, where we landed on short grass strips surrounded by mountains rising out of the jungle. It was bush flying for sure in Jim's Cessna-185, and there were five of us on board with full fuel tanks, so we were heavy. Jim knew his airplane and did a good job, but I was convinced he needed a higher performance aircraft for his circumstances.

Jim Blume's Cessna-185

The lush rainforest and mountain terrain we saw were indescribably beautiful, and I hoped the pictures I took would turn out well. I felt so privileged to see all we did that day! Jim said that we might be the last generation to see such scenes because of the rapid changes in the New Guinean culture. The many languages and dialects create communication barriers throughout the country. According to Jim there are about 800 languages and about 800 different dialects within those languages in New Guinea. Villages only a few miles apart often speak different languages or different dialects, although Pidgin is the common language of the country and is understood by most everyone.

Use of an airplane has certainly changed Jim's ministry! Our total flying time that day was one hour and fifteen minutes whereas riding in a truck and walking would have taken about four days. Nine-hour walks over the mountains and through the jungles to reach villages have been reduced to three minutes in the air. Villages are being reached with the airplane that otherwise might never be reached. I was utterly speechless at this knowledge, and I praised God for the privilege of this unique perspective and experience.

Approaching one of the villages, we walked across a river on a footbridge to visit a couple from New York and a nurse from England, who were working with the Peace Corps. On our way back to the airplane we were crossing the bridge with Jim in front of Rick and me following a short distance behind. When they got about halfway across, the bridge collapsed. I managed to step back off the bridge to safety, and Jim ran forward to the other side while Rick, clinging to the bridge, fell to the bottom and slammed against the bank on the other side. He was miraculously unhurt. I was able to walk down the riverbank, wade across the stream, and climb up the other side. Praise God, no one was hurt!

Pastor Scarberry on crashed bridge

Arriving back at the compound and Jim's home, we enjoyed an evening meal of chicken, *kaukau* (a kind of sweet potato), *pawpaw* (papaya), *pitpit* (an edible wild cane flower that grows rampantly in the country and looked kind of like a swamp cattail to me), cooked cabbage, and pineapple. All kinds of different fruit are readily available there, and I thoroughly enjoyed indulging. After the meal Rick washed the dishes then went out to play basketball. He was having a wonderful time playing basketball with the local teenage native boys, some of them from Wau Baptist church.

Jim and Mary's girls, Joy, eleven years old, and Lori, eight, tried to teach us Pidgin. I tried to learn a few words and recorded them in my travel diary:

lukim yu bihain = see you later;
Apinun = good afternoon;
gut moning = good morning;
mekim gen = do it over;
gut nait = good evening or good night.

We went to bed later that night and slept well in spite of Rick's loud snoring. On Wednesday we drove with Jim to Bulolo, a lumber and mining town of about 2000 people approximately ten miles northwest of Wau. Along the way we pulled off the road and stopped to look at a couple of huge, abandoned gold mining machines. The machines had been flown in, piece by piece, back in the 1920s by a joint venture between the US and Australia. Papua New Guinea is very rich in natural resources, including gold, oil, and chromium. The mining operation ceased when the Japanese came in during World War II.

Arriving in Bulolo, we visited one of Jim's national pastors at his church, which has about one hundred people in attendance. Jim had started and continues to look after about nine churches scattered throughout the jungles in small communities and pastored by national men that he is training. Some churches he visits every week, while others that are more established he visits once or twice a month.

Polygamy is openly practiced throughout the country of PNG. Men buy their wives, and the more wives a man owns, the more prestige and standing he has in his tribe. Girls are eligible for marriage at the age of twelve. Different tribes have different marriage customs. Among the Chimbu tribe, for instance, the more men girls have intimacy with before marriage, the more valuable they are. Pure communism is practiced within the clans or family groups, with everything held in common, and the women own the land within their clans. The people are not poor, though they seem to live poorly. It never ceases to amaze me how perverse and degraded a culture can be when God is left out of the equation and when the devil is in control.

That night's midweek service was in question because of the rain. Everyone there walked to church, so when it rained hard, people could not come. Fortunately, the rain stopped, and the service was held in Bulolo. We had a pretty good crowd, about 100 in attendance. Pastor Scarberry preached from Romans 13:14 and 2 Corinthians 5:20, expounding on how the world needs to see Christ in us. After the service and the drive back to Wau, Jim and I enjoyed some hangar flying and discussed plans to travel into Lewis Young's new landing strip to see his work, but it looked questionable at the time.

We had heard earlier that day that the New Guinean government had just changed the rules on airport approval to require all new runways to accommodate a twin-engine airplane. That meant that Lewis Young's new runway was too short to meet approval and would require building about an additional five hundred feet in length. This change was a real setback and disappointment to me. That runway had been built by the Awena village people using shovels, picks, and wheelbarrows. I could only imagine how Lewis felt, but we knew that God had a purpose. Since his runway had not yet been approved, we considered going in by helicopter on October 31. The Summer Institute of Linguistics (SIL) would take us in for 300 kina round trip, or about 256 US dollars.

The next day, while still at the Blumes' in Wau, we were up early discussing possibly walking back into Lewis's work on October 31. The SIL helicopter idea wasn't going to work, because the helicopter was in the maintenance shop for an inspection and would not be available until November 3. Rick wasn't interested in walking in, and if we did, time would be a little tight. In my physical condition, a six-hour walk from the nearest airstrip would probably take more like ten hours! At that point, I didn't know whether I would get to see Lewis or not.

Mary Blume and me at Wau market

THE OTHER WING

Jim Blume taught a Bible class once a week at the government school to students in grades seven through ten, and I was privileged to visit the class with him. All the girls were very neatly dressed in skirts and blouses or dresses, and the boys were dressed like little gentlemen. The students were very friendly and polite. The missionaries seemed to have freedom in some areas that we no longer have in the United States. They were free to teach through the Bible in all grade levels, which is no longer allowed in the USA, and Jim could conduct his Bible classes in any way he saw fit.

After lunch the Blumes took us to the market where the locals sold vegetables, sugar cane, coconut, and other produce. As we drove up, we saw a woman lying on the dirt in the parking area, not moving at all. We thought at first that she was asleep, so we got out to check on her, and she sat up, obviously very sick. She was also very pregnant. She fell over backward, moaned, foamed at the mouth, and then rolled over on the ground a couple of times. We thought she had died. We tried to find a pulse and detected her breathing. She eventually came to but seemed incoherent.

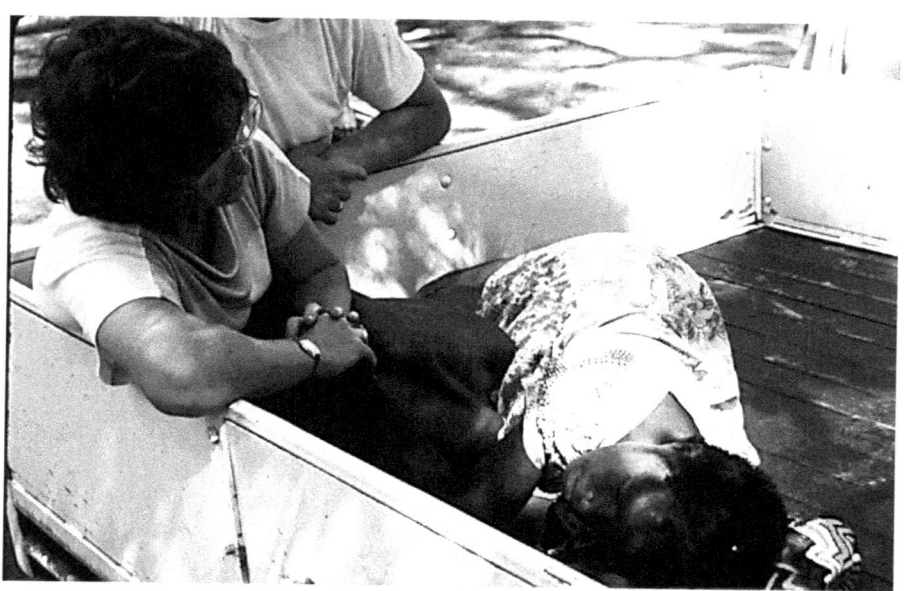

Mary Blume in truck with patient

We loaded the woman into the back of the pickup to take her to the hospital, but she tried to jump out, so Mary got in the back with her. We did finally get her to the hospital, where she fought us and didn't want to go in. She more than likely had had an epileptic fit, may have been going into labor, and was possibly demon possessed. Mary said that she knew the woman and that she was unmarried and mentally impaired. Men took advantage of her, and she had had other babies, one of which she had beaten almost to death, and another child which the clan had taken away from her. I felt so sorry for her, but we were helpless to do anything further.

Jim invited us to go in and see the hospital conditions. There were about ten to twelve beds in one room, which looked like 4x8 sheets of plywood with frames underneath. Only one had a two-inch foam rubber mattress with no cover on it. Family members had to provide any meals for their loved ones who were ill. The whole place seemed to be unkempt and dirty, in serious need of fresh, clean air.

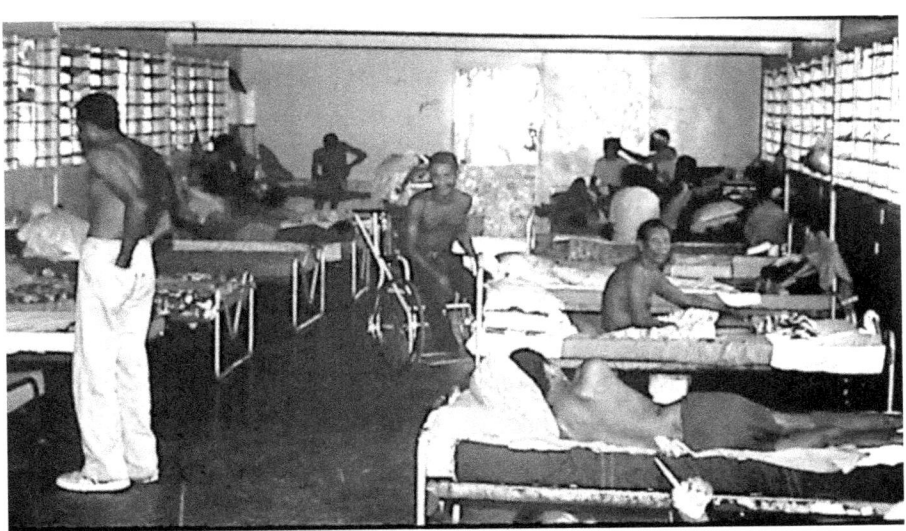

Hospital room in Wau

The terrain around Wau is beautiful. The city is surrounded by mountains rising out of the jungle with a beautiful river flowing through the area. However, the people have a very different work ethic from what we are accustomed to, working hard only if they see direct benefit to themselves. They would say, "You white men work hard all your lives in order to retire, and we are born retired."

The people seemed to take very little pride in their possessions, leaving tools and implements wherever they dropped them and showing little concern for cleanliness. I saw an older woman working in her garden topless that day, a common practice in the culture. Women also breastfeed openly in public and nobody seemed to think anything of it. Most of the people, however, did wear clothing, and some dressed really well.

Jim and Mary worked hard to show us a good time and make us comfortable. We all enjoyed our time there. We went to the Wau Ecological Institute, and while there were few animals there, all of them were native to Papua New Guinea, so it was interesting. We ate *kaukau*, *pitpit*, rice, and *pawpaw* for dinner that night—quite good!

After dinner we finally decided that the two missionary candidates who were in the area surveying for future ministry would walk to Lewis Young's work on the following Monday, October 31. The walk there and back would take four days. Our schedule had us leaving on November 4 to go back to Port Moresby, so Rick and I would not be able to go.

On Friday we were up early and prepared for our trip to the sizable city of Goroka. The weather was beautiful that morning as I made the takeoff in P2-SEQ, a Cessna-185. On the way to Goroka we flew over Lewis Young's area, where I asked Jim to take the controls while I took pictures of the airstrip that we had financed and the village where Lewis and his family served.

The airstrip sits on top of a mountain at approximately 6000 feet above a friendly looking little village area perched on the side of the mountain. About a hundred people ran up the mountain toward the, so far, unapproved strip, waving to us and thinking that we might land. The strip looked good. So it was a shame that we could not use it that day!

Captain Bob Warinner

Lewis Young's airstrip with village beyond

Airstrip in use after approval

Missionary Lewis Young, his two daughters, and villagers

We continued to Goroka and landed on a nice, paved runway. Goroka is the headquarters for the New Tribes Aviation ministry. Missionary Dan Peters picked us up, along with several other missionaries. Dan took us to his home to drop off our luggage. We then went out to lunch and had a wonderful time getting to know our new friends. Most of the missionaries there are with Baptist Bible Fellowship. When they knew we were coming, they planned a gathering to greet us. It was great to meet them, and have a precious time of fellowship together!

One of the missionaries in the group that I had the privilege of meeting was Terry Rowell, who had served in the Marine Corps and who had given his heart to Christ at the age of 26. The life transformation gave him the desire to attend Bible College in Springfield, Missouri, which eventually led him to the mission field of PNG. He had been serving in PNG for about ten years by that time. He talked me into playing chess with him, and we managed to keep games going until bedtime. He was a tough opponent, beating me most of the time.

The next morning, after time with the Lord, we all went golfing with Terry and had a great time, though none of us were very good. We went back to Dan Peter's, had a little lunch, and I had the opportunity to talk with Lewis Young on New Tribes' shortwave radio. He was disappointed that we had been unable to land on the airstrip. He was concerned that he might not be able to get the natives back to work on the runway to lengthen it. He planned to appeal the government's decision about the newly proposed rule. Thankfully, his airstrip was eventually approved without having to lengthen it.

That afternoon we headed to the airport for departure to visit missionary Frank Auterson, a missionary in the city of Kainantu, about 56 miles from Goroka. We arrived around 5:00 p.m., where Frank, his wife Karen, and two teenage boys Loyal and Lance met us.

I had started to come down with a cold the day before, and I felt horrible. The only place I wanted to be right then was home with my sweet wife to take care of me! Karen was good to me, though, and offered vitamin C and warm drinks. I went to bed earlier than many of the other nights, but slept poorly, blowing my nose and coughing all night. Fortunately, the Autersons had given me a room to myself.

The next day, which was Sunday, I went with Jim Blume to missionary Scott Carrier's small village ministry about a 45-minute drive away over rough, rutted dirt roads. The weather that day was beautiful and sunny, with the usual high humidity for the area. Scott was very sick with some kind of gastric problem that caused him extreme pain, so Peter Kolo, a native preacher boy and sweet Christian guy, went with us to the village ministry. We held a service, where Jim preached in Pidgin while Peter Kolo translated into their native tongue. When I gave a testimony, it was a three-way translation through Jim and Peter, from English to Pidgin to the native language.

This village and its people were as unkempt as any place I had ever seen. Abject poverty was the norm. Clothing was tattered and dirty, grass skirts were not uncommon, and some of the children were completely naked. Homes were humble one-room huts with woven bamboo walls, dirt floors, and grass roofs.

The people themselves were friendly, very curious and loved to have their picture taken. They were happy to see the missionaries again, and the children in particular surrounded us with shy smiles of welcome.

Jim and I peered into one hut where a woman sat on the floor before a fire with two little piglets at her side. Raising pigs was one of the main sources of income and an important food source among the people, so the people did all they could to keep the animals healthy and growing. I was told that sometimes the women would nurse the piglets if necessary to keep them alive.

Scott Carrier's village ministry outreach

After the service the rest of the group went out to dinner in Kainantu, and I stayed home to rest, still feeling terrible with my cold. I did feel better after a little rest which enabled me to attend the evening service in Kainantu, where Rick was preaching.

I slept better that night and was able to get up early on Monday. After devotions we had breakfast and made plans to fly to Mount Hagon, where Terry Rowell ministered. Before leaving, I stopped at the Summer Institute of Linguistics store to get something for my cold. SIL has a whole community there—store, hospital, body shop, lumber mill—you name it— about 500 people live within this compound, mainly SIL employees, missionaries, and their families. SIL had been given the land by the PNG government in an attempt to keep two warring tribes from having constant conflicts with one another.

We finally left the compound around 4 p.m. and arrived in Mount Hagon about an hour later, where Terry Rowell met us. Mount Hagon, a large highland city, has a very nice airport with a control tower, paved runways, and other such amenities. Mission Aviation Fellowship (MAF) has a fixed base operation (FBO) there, offering fuel, flight training, charters, and related services.

The next day, Tuesday, Terry wanted to fly out to Tari, a large government patrol post in the Western Highlands, to survey the area. He planned to move up there, build a house, minister in the area, and start a church. We could not land in the area where we wanted to, about 15 miles north of Tari, because the landing strip was private, belonging to the Wesleyans, and the airstrip was a little short for our load. Written permission was required to use a private strip, which of course we did not have. We circled the area several times, so Terry was able to assess the village surroundings in preparation for his future ministry there.

Common sight in Tari

We then flew to the Tari airport, landed, walked around in Tari for a couple of hours, entered a store or two, bought cold sodas, and went back to the airplane. Tari was much more primitive than anything we had seen so far, especially in dress. The men had painted faces and bones in their noses and wore grass skirts that covered their front and leaves covering their buttocks. Women wore grass skirts and went topless. Most of the people we had seen in other places had been dressed completely in some fashion, even though many were very dirty and tattered, but at least they were clothed.

I slept well that night and felt like I was on the mend the next day. After breakfast we went to look at Terry Rowell's Bible college, or, as he lovingly called it, the "Rice Seminary." It was just a little bamboo hut on the back of his lot. Two preacher boys sleep there, and he taught them at a little table each morning. It seemed that some of God's greatest work was taking place in the uttermost parts of the earth.

Rice Seminary

Afterward Terry took us downtown to a Christian book store. As we were leaving the store, an older man dressed in a grass skirt and a suit coat that was so dirty that it could have stood by itself, approached me wanting to sell me a handmade tray. (The custom in many countries is to barter over the price of an item until an agreement is reached.) He wanted 12 kina, or about 10 US dollars for it. Terry asked him what his second or number two price was, and he said 10 kina plus 50 toea

(10.50). I told him that was too much; I didn't want it. We walked out to Terry's truck, but the man followed us and made an offer. We haggled a little bit, and he finally said, "Okay." Satisfied with his sale he walked away with 7 kina, or about 6 US dollars in exchange for the tray. We went back to the airport and took off to return to Wau and Blume's home. It was a beautiful flight! Over the course of our time in Papua New Guinea I had come to deeply appreciate Jim Blume in so many ways. He is a man of God who loves those people!

As we sat for supper that night, some natives came to the door wanting to sell us bows and arrows. I have always been interested in archery. I was fascinated with their handmade bows and arrows and wanted to take a bow and some arrows home as souvenirs. The price was right: 50 toea for each arrow or about 45 cents US; 1 kina for fancy ones; and 5 kina for the bow, so we bought some. One of the men from the church came to the door and gave us each an arrow as a gift, and the wife of the native pastor of the church Jim established in Wau had left us each a *bilum*, a kind of stretchy bag that reminded me of a shopping bag. The locals load up the large bags, place the handles around their foreheads, and carry the load resting on their backs. It is amazing the amount they carry that way.

Lady using a bilum to carry her goods

We went off to the midweek service in the Blumes' pickup, with the men, women, and children in the back box. About 230 people came to the service. Pastor Scarberry sang a solo, and I preached from 2 Corinthians 5:14–20. At the invitation one young girl came forward for salvation. Praise the Lord! The church also decided to give us a love offering, which amounted to 43 kina. These people had sacrificed to express their appreciation for us. What a blessing and honor that was! Jim told us that they had never done anything like that before. After the service we had a good time with those who stayed around for fellowship. The pastor's wife gave me another *bilum,* and another member of the church in Wau gave each of us two more arrows as gifts.

We knew our time together was coming to a close. It had been such a precious experience that I would never forget. People everywhere love to be loved and given attention. Everyone had been such a blessing to us, and I knew that we had blessed and encouraged them also. My heart may have been longing for home, but it is still always so hard to say goodbye! I was still coughing and fighting the cold somewhat on Thursday when Jim flew us to Port Moresby for our scheduled departure on Friday, assuming the flight was operating. We had packed our bows in PVC pipe, hoping the airline would allow us to carry them on. We weren't too hopeful, because the pipes were pretty long, but we didn't want to lose them by checking them.

The weather was high-scattered clouds as we got in the air and over the first ridge from Wau. On our flight we were able to see a couple more village landing strips that Jim used for ministry. The terrain was very rugged, with dense jungle. I often wondered what we would do if the engine failed. Chances of survival would be next to zero except for God's grace. I guess that is true for each day, no matter what we are doing. "*My times* are *in thy hand........*" *Psalm 31:15*

In Port Moresby we went to the Aviation Aerodrome Operations Department and talked to the head man, Gordon Howell, regarding Lewis Young's setback due to the new runway approval policies. Mr. Howell was an Australian man, 73 years old with 22,000 hours of flight time. He invited me to join the department, but I explained to him that my calling was to serve the Lord in a ministry I started called Wings As Eagles. Mr. Howell said that he was concerned about aviation safety and that the accident rate had been way too high. He was determined to do something about it and said that it had to start somewhere; Lewis just happened to get caught in the crossfire. Mr. Howell wanted runways to be at least 600 meters long, with no more than a 10-degree gradient. He said the natives were innocent people and that his department had to watch out for them.

An example of the dangers of flight in PNG

We left for the airport in Port Moresby about 9:00 a.m., stopping on the way to see another missionary in the area, Ken Lyndsy, his wife, and their son Ken. While there, a couple of other missionaries drove in, Joe Hagen and John Gray. Joe is an Australian that plays the harmonica, who promised to send me a tape of his playing. He used to play in bars before he gave his life to Christ. Now his music brings glory to God.

A few months back he had been attacked by five guys, knocked down with a 2x4, which broke some of his ribs. Fighting for his life, although not a very big man, he managed to get to his feet and hit one of the men with an uppercut to the jaw. It was so hard that it lifted the guy off the ground, knocked his teeth out, broke his jaw, and gave him a concussion. As John's assailant lay unconscious and broken, his assailant's buddies picked him up and left. John believed that God gave him supernatural power that day to defend himself.

After a relatively brief visit with these missionaries, we were off to the airport to send Jim on his way home before the weather got bad in Wau. We checked in at Continental and found out they were operating on time. Since they would not allow us to carry on our PVC-packed bows, we checked them as far as Guam. Only about 30 people were on board, and I thought that unless the airline was making their revenue on cargo, this trip probably would not operate much longer.

After our plane took off, I looked down on Papua New Guinea, reflecting on the past weeks. So many people there seemed to live in a literal prison, with fences, bars, and mean dogs. The bone through the nose indicates initiation into manhood. A woman can be purchased by a man to be his wife. Taking belongings that others had failed to secure is not theft, since that would indicate the original owner doesn't want them, or they would have been sure to secure them. It was appalling to see firsthand a culture where God was never honored and Bible principles were never followed. Left to themselves, people fall into the devil's path of depravity and destruction without hope either in this world or the next.

I also reflected on the challenge of ministering to people living in such a culture, and what a blessing it was to meet and minister, if only for a brief time, with some of God's choicest servants on the field of Papua New Guinea. It takes a special calling to special people who will be obedient to God's call to reach out to people in what might seem to be hopeless circumstances, freely and faithfully giving them the gospel of Jesus Christ and the opportunity to trust him for salvation. Then patiently teaching them from the Scriptures through the years.

I thought with awe and almost disbelief that I had had the privilege of being there in Papua New Guinea for almost two weeks. The privilege of traveling to remote villages, helping the missionaries in their ministries, observing unusual dress and customs and eating new foods, praying for needs and for souls to be saved, and being changed by all I had done and seen. I praised God for his wonderful goodness. Had I not said, "Yes, Lord, here am I; send me," I could never have had this experience. Now we were bound for Australia and for the second part of our amazing adventure!

12

Down Under

"To preach the gospel in the regions beyond. . . .
— Corinthians 10:16

After leaving Port Moresby, PNG, we came to our first stop in Guam. We went to claim our bows and discovered that they had not arrived. Pastor Scarberry became rather irritated because we had checked five items since leaving Minneapolis, and all had been lost! We asked an agent to go look for them personally, which he did, and in his search, he found the bows. They had been placed in the wrong container when removed from the airplane. We rechecked the bows to Honolulu, and were assigned the last two seats on the plane.

Arriving in Honolulu, we called the Pacific Marina Hotel for a room. The hotel van picked us up, and we settled into our room for a rest, hoping to get on the flight to Sydney, Australia, very early Saturday morning. We had left Guam Friday evening, November 4, and arrived in Honolulu early Friday morning, November 4, because we had crossed the international date line.

We were tired after traveling all night so turned in to get a little sleep. After getting up later that morning we went to Pearl Harbor. The boats to the memorial were not operating because of unsettled weather and high winds. We were able to watch a film instead, then looked around a bit and caught the bus back to the airport to check on a place to store our bows and other gifts while we visited Australia for the next eight days. The airport wanted five dollars per day per item. Ouch! But we didn't want to carry all these things to Australia, so we asked the hotel if they would store our things for us. Thankfully they said that they would.

Praise the Lord! With that problem solved, we trusted that everything would be there when we returned.

I called our daughter Sharon in Owatonna, Minnesota, wanting to know where Juanita was and found her there. Sharon was tickled to hear from me and expressed her love about four times before handing the phone to Juanita. It is such a great blessing to be loved by your children! It was good to talk to my wife and sweetheart again. I certainly missed her and wished she could have been with me. In fact, I would have loved to have had the whole family along!

We went to the airport to check in for our departure, only to discover that the flight would be at least four hours late. At 2:30 a.m. we found out that the flight was full. Riding space-available has its trials, but the price is right! So, it was back to the hotel and to bed for the rest of the night.

Since flying out the next day didn't look good, we caught a bus to Waikiki to do some sightseeing. We went to the international marketplace where Rick did some Christmas shopping for his family, followed by some walking and a buffet dinner before taking the bus back to Honolulu. Back at the airport we boarded the plane and were placed in business class. Finally, we were on our way to Australia. Praise the Lord!

Our trip to Australia was the desire of Rick's heart, to visit and to personally acquaint himself with the work and ministry of a former Bible college classmate, whom he and his church faithfully supported. He, of course, hoped to encourage the missionary, his family, and the church as well.

We lost our Sunday while traveling when we crossed the international date line again, arriving in Sydney on Monday morning at 7 a.m. We cleared customs, and Pastor Ken Burdett, his former Bible college classmate and pastor of Berean Baptist Church in Penrith, picked us up and drove us around a little. We stopped by the Bible college where Pastor Burdett served as dean under Marvin Matthews, the president of the college. From there we went to Penrith, about a 30-minute drive, and toured his church building before driving to his home, where we met his wife Nora and their teenage sons Shawn and Scott.

Shawn is limited mentally, and the Burdetts and I soon connected over the challenges that our families shared as we raised our sons. Before long we were all in tears as I told them about our experiences with Gerald. I also told them about the Shepherds Baptist Ministries (now Shepherds Ministries), a home that cares for Christian adults who cannot live on their own and where we had placed Gerald in 1984. Shepherds was a godsend beyond words for Gerald and our family. Gerald continues to do well at Shepherds as he lives and works there where he is needed, feeling useful and fulfilled in his life.

The Burdetts obviously loved Shawn dearly and were very sensitive toward him. They were interested in Shepherds, not having heard of it before, but recognizing that the time would come when Shawn would need a place to live outside of their home. They were dear people, and Nora reminded me of my sister Mary Lou who is now with the Lord.

Scott, Ken, Nora, and Shawn Burdett and Rick Scarberry

I slept well that night and woke up thanking the Lord that my cold was just about over! It was good to feel healthy again. Pastor Burdett and Nora wanted to take us on a tour of Sydney, so we took the subway to the central area of town on the waterfront. We enjoyed a beautiful cruise around the bay area at a cost of 11 dollars each. This area reminded me a lot of Seattle or Vancouver in the Pacific Northwest. After the cruise we went to the Waterfront Restaurant and to a beautiful two-story shopping mall with a large hanging clock that spanned both floors. The clock had been presented to Australia by England's Queen Elizabeth in celebration of the country's bicentennial. Every hour on the hour from 9:00 a.m. to 10:00 p.m. it plays music and shows six historical stage-like scenes through a glass window. After several hours at the mall we took a tram to the central business district

Shopping mall clock

In the central business district, we went up into the Sydney Tower, also known as the Space Needle, where the view of the harbor and city was spectacular! Pastor Burdett had never been up in the tower before, so we all enjoyed it together for the first time. We took the subway back to the restaurant for our dinner. It was a rather classy place and very expensive, but it was very good! From our table we had a view of the bay area where we could see a showboat and lots of other traffic. After dinner we walked to the subway and rode the two hours back to Penrith and then took a taxi home, where I wrote and studied until late that evening. I really missed my wife that day and wished she could have been there to share all these new experiences.

Sydney, Australia

The next day we went back to the Bible college, located on the east side of Sydney. We visited sitting in the teacher's lounge for a while, and then I went with Nora to her class and shared with her girls' class a little about our lives and Proverbs 31. After I spoke for a short time I sat in the class while three of the students each gave a sample Sunday school lesson. Nora was a good teacher, and I could tell the students loved her. We had lunch at the college and then went back to the house to relax for a while. Pastor Burdett wanted to make some structural changes to the church by removing a wall and adding a couple others. So we went to the church with him that afternoon to help with that project.

We went home for dinner, visited, and played UNO before we went to bed. Pastor Burdett had asked me to preach for him on Sunday morning, sing in the chapel on Friday, preach and sing the following Sunday evening. I didn't feel capable, but I said I'd do it, trusting God to give me his enabling grace and use me in some way to be a blessing.

Nora fixed a great breakfast for us the next morning, and Pastor Burdett took us golfing. I am not very good at golf, but we had a good time together. Later we went back to the church to continue the wall framing project. By about 6:30 we had finished all that we could do and went home where Nora had fixed leg of lamb for dinner. Pastor Burdett wanted to run some errands and do a little shopping that evening. The shops there are open only one night a week and closed on Sunday. No shopping on Sunday was a law the government was trying to do away with, but it was being resisted by the people. Would to God such laws remain in effect today in the USA! Like in Papua New Guinea, public schools in Australia are open to religious instruction once a week.

After shopping we went back home, played UNO again until about midnight, and then were off to bed. I had to admit that I was wearing out and becoming eager to go home. Everyone had been very hospitable and sweet to us, and it was a great blessing for us to be used by God, to be a blessing to others, and to share the gospel, but my home was pulling at my heartstrings.

The next morning, Friday, I was up early and off to the Bible college for chapel and my solo. I still had a slight tickle in my throat, but with the Lord's help I thought I would be able to sing that day. I practiced the song "Down from His Glory" for the chapel service with a young accompanist, Mark Western, who really knew what he was doing on the piano! Pastor Scarberry preached "Don't Quit." He was a good preacher and put a lot of God-guided humor into his preaching that engaged his listeners in a positive way.

After lunch at the school we went home to change clothes and head for a visit to the bush country with Alick and Shirley Robertson, a couple from the church. Alick was from Snowy River and worked for the Sydney Water Board, so he had access to government land that few other people had. He said that we were the first Americans to set foot on some of that land. The Robertsons were hospitable people and seemed genuinely glad to take us out. We rode everywhere in a Toyota 4x4 Land Cruiser, looking for interesting birds and animals. On our bush tour we saw kangaroos (they called them 'roos) by the hundreds: wallaroo, wallaby, and rock wallaby—all different types of kangaroos. We also saw a ringtail possum in a tree with a little one, called a joey. Alick had told me that I wouldn't be able to shake them out of the tree, so of course I shook the tree, and they came tumbling down! At the same moment I lost my footing and fell backward down a small hill. Fortunately, I was not hurt. When we saw a herd of brumbies—wild horses—I knew my daughter Sharon would be jealous when she found out. We saw a young emu, a bird a lot like an ostrich, and a goanna, a huge lizard-like creature about six to eight feet long, sitting still on its way up a large tree.

Brumbies

Alick had a cookout for us in the bush and fixed T-bone steak, *snags* or sausage, baked potatoes, bread, salad, billy tea, and cake. Billy tea is a tea unique to Australia. The tea leaf is placed in a bucket of hot water, and the bucket is swung in a circle, causing the centrifugal force to bring out the flavor of the tea leaves. If you like tea, it is great! What a feast we enjoyed!

Alick making billy tea (above) and steaks (right)

Alick had a bright spotlight that we used to find wildlife after darkness fell. We saw several wombats, wild, pig-like animals that come out at night; I tried to catch one with no success. We also chased rabbits that night and tried to catch them too, but of course we failed. Up in a tree we saw a greater glider possum with a long bushy tail and a really cute face. The greater glider possums commonly live in old hollowed-out trees, look like fluffy teddy bears, and can soar as much as 300 feet in the air from tree to tree. The drive back to the Burdetts' at night was uneventful, but it had been a full day, and we were all ready for a good night's rest.

On Sunday, November 13, I woke up earlier than usual and began to pray and meditate over the message Pastor Burdett had invited me to preach that morning. I always feel so humbled and incapable, but I claim the promise of God from Philippians 4:13 that *"I can do all things through Christ which strengtheneth me."* I was on my knees praying for the day's services, my family, and others for a good while. I reviewed my Scripture text, then prepared to leave for church. I sang "God Did a Wonderful Thing for Me," and I once again preached on "Saved for Service" from 2 Corinthians 5:14–21. I got many positive comments, and Pastor Burdett and Nora seemed to be blessed by the message. I praise the Lord for His enabling grace. *"Not unto us, O Lord, not unto us, but unto thy name give glory, for thy mercy, and for thy truth's sake." Psalm 115:1*

After the service we enjoyed a delicious scalloped potato dinner. Nora really did a great job of caring for her guests. Pastor Burdett and Nora left after dinner to make a couple of visits to church members, one at the hospital and another to a couple that had just given birth to a baby girl.

Rick had preached at Pastor Matthew's church that morning, and was brought back to the Burdetts' about that afternoon, and we visited until Pastor Burdett and Nora returned later, reminding us that church started at 6:00 p.m. We quickly changed clothes and left for church. Rick wanted us to sing "Beulah Land" as a trio, along with Nora, but I didn't know the song, so he and Nora sang it as a duet. I then sang the song "Why" as a solo. Rick preached, again with a lot of humor. Nora laughed heartily at some of his anecdotes that painted amusing pictures in our minds. After the service the church people had a fellowship and what they call supper. Australians traditionally eat five times a day: breakfast, morning tea, lunch, afternoon tea (which is our supper), and then supper (which would be our bedtime snack).

The church gave us a love offering, which we in turn gave to Ken to help them out. They had gone overboard to take care of us and show us a good time. At church Alick gave me a can of billy tea to take back with me and introduced me to his son and his son's girlfriend. After the church fellowship, we went home and enjoyed visiting while playing Skip-Bo until late.

On Monday, November 14, Pastor Burdett took us to Katoomba, a tourist town in the Blue Mountains, a very beautiful place where he showed us a number of sights and took us on a train ride down a mountain side. It had to be a 45-degree incline, and we were told that it is the steepest pitch for a rail line in the world.

Pastor Scarberry and me on the Katoomba Scenic Railway

We went back to the house to prepare to leave for home. It had been a wonderful experience, but, glory to God, I was antsy to get home! Nora had fixed us a memorable going away meal with trout that Alick had given her to cook for us, and she went all out and bought lobster and fixed it also. It was beautifully done.

The drive to the Sydney airport took us about an hour and twenty minutes. We checked in and were assigned seats right away, which was a wonderful answer to prayer. I was given a seat in first class, and Rick was given a seat in coach. The flight attendant was holding strictly to the book and would not allow him in first class even to visit. Since Rick had gotten a little taste of the better treatment on our previous flights, I think he was a little disappointed. However, as a passenger traveling on a former employee companion pass, he was technically restricted to being seated in coach, though most flight attendants did not usually hold to that rule if there was space available in first class. However, it was still a good deal, no matter how we looked at it. I will always be thankful for the privilege of flying on those passes. I leaned back in my first-class seat and slept for a while. We were scheduled into Honolulu early in the morning.

We arrived in Honolulu on schedule within two hours before our flight for San Francisco. I called Pacific Marina Hotel, and about 30 minutes later they delivered to us the items we had put in storage. We got everything taped up and ready to check on the flight. The load was fairly light, and it was looking good for us to get on the flight. Amen! The gate agent asked Rick to change his shirt, which he did. He was not sloppily dressed but was wearing a pullover type shirt. The airline industry has a nonrevenue dress code that consists of sharp-looking slacks and a button-up shirt for men. We were then assigned seats in the coach section and were able to sit together.

We arrived in San Francisco, and just as I was leaving the men's room after the flight, Rick caught me and told me there was a flight boarding for Denver. We rushed to the counter, and, sure enough, that particular flight had been delayed a little, and there were seats available, so we were quickly on our way to Denver. As we arrived in Denver, an earlier flight to Minneapolis was also delayed just long enough for us to get on, so we boarded and were headed to Minneapolis.

I had tried calling Juanita at her mother's before leaving Denver, but there was no answer. Upon arrival in Minneapolis, I called again, and this time she picked up the phone. Our luggage had not made the early flight with us, so we had to wait for the next flight, which was carrying our luggage. All our checked items eventually arrived in good condition.

We were so thankful for the way the Lord worked things that day. It was almost unbelievable—only God! We had left Sydney at 5:30 p.m. on November 14 and, crossing the international date line yet once again, arrived in Minneapolis at 10:45 p.m. the same day. God had worked a miracle to enable us to travel such a long distance, unexpectedly make several connecting flights, and arrive home in such a short time!

Mrs. Scarberry arrived a couple hours later to pick up her husband, loaded up and drove back to Superior, Wisconsin. That night. Juanita and I got to bed at her mother's in the very early hours of the morning. It had been a very long day, but I was so very glad to be back.

The next day we got up and called our daugthers Cindy and Sharon before we headed for home. As there was a storm coming our way, we wasted no time. We pulled up at our home in Park Rapids just as the sleet and snow started, and that night we got about six inches of snow. One day's delay, or even a few hours, and we would have had trouble getting home for another few days. God is so good!

To this day I thank God for the awesome privilege of that tremendous trip. The world's needs are far beyond our comprehension! *Lord, please help me to do what I can to reach the lost! Cause me to be faithful!*

God couldn't have given me anyone more congenial and pleasant to travel with than Rick. He became a good friend, and his church, Twin Ports. Rick resigned his pastorate at Twin Ports and took a church in Indiana. A few years later, while playing basketball with some of his young men, his heart failed. He had met that appointment mentioned in Hebrews 9:27, and awoke in his long-awaited home in heaven. It was a sad day for his family and those left behind. As Ecclesiastes 9:12 reminds us, none of us is guaranteed another day. *"For man also knoweth not his time........ "* We must be ready for the moment God calls us home! And Pastor Scarberry certainly was ready, for he had trusted the Lord Jesus Christ as his personal Savior, trusting Christ alone to save him from his sin and receive him into glory when this life was done. In the time that I knew Rick, he had a passion to live for God and loved to share the good news of salvation with everyone he could, at home and around the world. Praise God for his faithful testimony!

13

God Builds a Team

"For we are labourers together with God......."
—*1 Corinthians 3:9*

A couple of months later I flew to Jerseyville, Illinois, to meet Doug Kalapp and take him on our arranged mission trip to Mexico. He was waiting for me as I taxied in, and I sensed an immediate connection between us, even before the moment we shook hands. He took me to his home to meet his family, to get to know each other and enjoy some time together as brothers and sisters in the Lord. The next morning, we met with the other pastor who was to join us, loaded up, took to the skies, heading for Jimenez and the work of missionary Lanny Ashcraft. Arriving in Nuevo Laredo, Mexico, across the border from Laredo, Texas, we cleared Mexican customs, refueled, and were airborne again for Jimenez.

Upon our arrival in Jimenez, Lanny was there to pick us up and was excited to see us. After the evening meal we got settled into a local hotel. As we climbed into our beds, almost instantaneously our preacher friend began to snore loudly. Doug and I could hardly believe it. Not even Rick Scarberry could have rivaled that! We began to laugh, and since we couldn't go to sleep with that commotion going on, we talked and shared our vision until about midnight. I don't think the snoring ever did stop that night.

The next morning Lanny picked up the three of us in Jimenez and drove us to his home located on several acres west of Jimenez. We enjoyed a nice Mexican breakfast and discussed plans for the week of gospel outreach. Over the course of that week we held several open-air services, with Lanny preaching and doing his magic illustrations, or translating for one of us as we preached. Our hearts were greatly blessed as a number of souls trusted Christ as Savior. There is an openness to the gospel in Mexico that is uncommon in the United States today, and I believe one reason is because of their poverty. The people there recognize their inability to meet their needs without the hand of God, but because of our material abundance and seemingly infinite choices, we feel we can care for ourselves and have little need. At week's end, Lanny took us to the airstrip along with several of his church members. We boarded the airplane for our return flight with hearts overflowing, rejoicing over what God had allowed us to experience and have a part in.

A few months later, in June 1989, Doug Kalapp resigned his church and joined the Wings as Eagles ministry. God had answered my prayer, and we were now a team, with the fully surrendered support of our wives. I don't think Doug, his dear wife Karen, or their four children had a true picture of the sacrifice this new ministry was going to be, but they were soon to find out.

The Kalapp family: Kim, David, Allison, Jonathan, Doug, and Karen

By now it had become clear to us that it was time to sell the resort in order to give ourselves completely to the ministry. Four of our children were now married, and Gerald had been placed at Shepherds Baptist Ministries in Union Grove, Wisconsin. So Juanita and I were empty nesters once again. The resort had been a wonderful place for us, our family, and so many others. God had used it in a mighty way. Though it was hard in some ways to give it up, God was once again moving us in a different direction and into a new and exciting phase of our life's journey. It was again time to submit to his clear, plain path.

Doug and his family desperately needed a vehicle to travel in. We had accepted a motorhome and a late model Ford F-150 pickup as partial payment for the resort. Juanita and I had planned on traveling in the motorhome ourselves, but the two of us could travel in the Ford and stay in homes, prophet's chambers, or motels much more easily than the Kalapp family. Therefore, we delivered the motorhome to the Kalapps where they lived in Jerseyville with the understanding that should the Lord someday bless them abundantly with resources, they would pay us for it. As a result, they began their deputation schedule.

Doug began to call independent Baptist pastors, and God opened the doors to about 150 meetings the first year, where he presented the Wings ministry and encouraged and organized mission trips.

We bought a small used travel trailer and parked it at Dennis and Lee Deneaus' place in Park Rapids as our home while we sought the Lord's leading on where he would have us relocate.

Shortly thereafter, Juanita and I were scheduled for a mission conference at Rock of Ages Prison Ministry in Tennessee. We drove the pickup, and the Lord put it in my mind about taking along the title. We were learning to listen for and be obedient to the urgings of the Holy Spirit of God, and God blessed that in such wonderful ways! As we got acquainted with other people attending the conference, one of the Rock of Ages missionaries approached me about our vehicle. He had been pulling his travel trailer with an older van and expressed to me his need for a pickup. After a little discussion we swapped vehicles; I signed the title over to him, and we left the conference with his van. Juanita and I spent many miles driving and many nights sleeping in that van in between meetings.

The Kalapps were really struggling with the six of them living in a 22-foot cabover motorhome, so they bought a 12-foot sleeper trailer to pull behind. Someone gave them a camper shell that Doug and Karen used for their personal bedroom while at their home base. That is how they lived for at least two and a half years. They left Jerseyville and joined a Baptist church in Hammond, Indiana. When they were not on the road or when Doug was with me on a mission trip, they would park behind the college gym.

Kalapps' temporary home

Reflecting on their time just after saying yes to the Lord and joining Wings As Eagles, Mrs. Kalapp wrote the following article for a Christian ladies' publication:

We sold almost everything we had—our home and all of our furniture. We went on the road to raise support and literally had to pray, *Give us this day our daily bread*. But God showed us he was faithful, and he taught me so much about faith and his faithfulness. Our older son David says those seven months we traveled together are his favorite childhood memories because we all learned how God would take care of us, and we were all together all of the time. In one of our first churches, I prayed all through Sunday school and church that God would provide my four children with a Sunday meal, petrified that God would let us starve! A man came up to my husband and gave him $40 and told him to take us out to eat. That was just the beginning of many answers to prayer and ways God showed us he loved us and would take care of us.

During the two winters that we were there [parked behind the gym], it got so cold that the pipes would freeze, and the boys had to haul [drinking and cooking] water from the gym, where we took our showers. I dreamed of what it would be like to again just have an indoor bathroom and not have to walk outside (sometimes in rain and mud) to take a shower or go to the bathroom.

Doug's wife Karen was an example of a submissive, supportive wife, and ministry helper as described in the Scriptures. Doug stayed busy presenting the ministry and putting mission trips together, which kept me busy flying the trips, sometimes twice a month.

In the early part of our ministry together, Doug and I were in Bowie, Texas, spending some quality time with Dr. Frazer of Bearing Precious Seed, who had been so very instrumental in God's leading in my life and ministry, by challenging me to become the other wing and thereby encouraging us to launch the Wings As Eagles ministry.

The airport operator in Bowie had a Piper Aztec for sale. It had a fresh paint job and carried six people plus baggage. He was interested in our Beech Debonair. I took the Aztec for a test flight, and after seeking God's wisdom and direction, we negotiated a deal and ended up leaving the Debonair in Texas and flying the Aztec home. It was a little hard to say goodbye to what had been our family airplane and the airplane that had launched the Wings ministry, but it was time to move on. Now we had an airplane that could carry five besides myself. God's provision was again so evident. Doug and I flew many mission trips in the Aztec with pastors and lay people to Mexico, the Dominican Republic, the Caicos Islands, and Canada.

Just a few short years after choosing to say yes to the Lord and launch the other wing, calling it Wings As Eagles Mission Air Service, I had been given the privilege of serving the Lord in countries around the world that I had only read about before. We serve an amazing God!

Juanita and me with the Aztec

14

Central America

"My little children, let us not love in word, neither in tongue; but in deed and in truth."—1 John 3:18

I had become acquainted with an organization called Good Samaritan Baptist Ministries, headquartered in Villa Rica, Georgia, and headed up by Bob and Joan Tyson, with ministries located in San Marcos de Colon, Honduras, a city on the border with Nicaragua. On January 15, 1991, I left on a survey trip to San Marcos to meet the Tysons and to get acquainted with the Good Samaritan Baptist Ministries. I flew on a Continental airline pass to Tegucigalpa, Honduras, arriving in Tegucigalpa in the early afternoon. After I went through customs I felt lost. There was no one there to meet me that I could immediately find, and the natives were surrounding me, trying to take my bags out of my hands to carry them for me, for a fee of course; others tried to take me to a taxi; and still more tried to exchange my money. I had never been accosted quite like that before, and I was beginning to get a little nervous when a Honduran man approached me holding a piece of paper with my name on it. His name was George, and thankfully he was my driver. Since he could speak only a few words of English, and I knew next to no Spanish, our travels for the next three hours were rather silent.

George drove like a mad man in his Nissan pickup, passing on blind uphill curves and performing other hair-raising maneuvers. Upon arriving in the city of Choluteca, about 34 miles west of San Marcos, I met my driver's family, sweet, friendly people. We then drove over to a motel to meet missionary Bob Tyson, who was having a meeting there with his national pastors. It was great to see a familiar face at long last!

I learned from Bob Tyson that George had been saved for about 18 years. He was from Nicaragua and had been in Honduras about 11 years. George took me to Tysons' home in San Marcos de Colon, and shortly afterwards we drove back to Choluteca for an evening service at an established church. An American missionary by the name of John Nelms preached, and I gave a testimony. Three people trusted Christ in that service—glory to God!

Bob and Joan Tyson

On the way back to San Marcos that night, about 10:30 p.m., we came upon a man lying in the middle of the road. We swerved to miss him and drove on. Bob Tyson felt that it was probably a set up to get us to stop and then be robbed. Upon arrival in San Marcos that night, I stayed with Bob Tyson's son Phillip, his wife, and their four-month-old baby Stephany.

At that time the Tysons had active works in both Honduras and Nicaragua, starting churches, operating Feed the Hungry program, and running a school program they called Opportunity of a Lifetime. They asked people from the US to support a child in school for 30 dollars per month. Juanita and I took on the support of 14-year-old Lorena until she graduated. After graduation, Lorena married a doctor, and we have always been grateful for the opportunity to invest in her life. We later took my sisters Bette and Rosalie to San Marcos, Honduras, to visit the work there, and they both supported students as well. Neither of them had ever before been on a mission trip. Their hearts were so blessed that they have never gotten over it!

Sisters Bette and Rose and me with Honduran girl

On my second day in Honduras I visited the Feed the Hungry kitchens, school office, and school adoption program, all very impressive works. In the evening we went back to Choluteca for a service, where John Nelms preached again, with six trusting Christ. The crowd was a little smaller this time because of the attack on Iraq, which was the start of the Desert Storm war, and concern about the lights going out. It had been announced that to conserve fuel, electricity for lighting might be cut off. Fuel was being rationed to two gallons per car per gas station. We went back to San Marcos after the service and watched what news we could get. Of course, imaginations ran wild, and I began to feel a little lonely to get home.

The third day we went to Ocotal, Nicaragua, just a few miles away, to visit a church and school that was under Bob Tyson's watch care. I couldn't believe the length of time it took to get across the border! There were three different check points about a mile and a half apart that we had to clear leaving Honduras, and then two or three getting into Nicaragua. But it was worth it all, for we were well received by the people, and our visit was a real blessing. I met a 53-year-old man, Ruben, who spoke English. He had been saved but had no Bible. I felt so bad that I did not have a Bible to give him at that time, and I promised to get him one of each in Spanish and English.

The next day we went to San Lucas, Nicaragua, a little town of about a thousand people. We visited an active work there of about 120 people pastored by a national. Their custom in a church service is for the men to sit on one side of the church, the women on the other, and the children outside.

In San Lucas we met a high-ranking commander for the Sandinistas, a violent group that overthrew the President of Nicaragua in 1979 and persecuted Christians and burned their houses. He had just come home from spending time in Cuba. He had trusted Christ as Savior just 20 days before, and God had dramatically changed his heart in that miraculous way that only God can.

That day we also visited Victoria Baptist Church and Pastor Elieso Maleno in a remote mountain area. Bob had led Elieso to Christ and baptized him 16 years earlier. Elieso was now 34 years old and regularly walked four miles from his home to pastor about 75 people. He also pastored a small mission work elsewhere on the mountain where 13 people had recently given their hearts to Christ.

We were privileged to make a visit to Bet el (Bethel) Baptist Church in the middle of nowhere. The pastor was paid five dollars a month and raised corn and a few other crops to exist. He had approximately 75 people in his church, with many of his people walking several miles to the services. He also had a nearby mission work with about 10 believers in Christ. When that work was solid enough, they planned to call a pastor, and Pastor Maleno would then start another mission work. These men are amazing, with hearts that deeply love the Lord!

After a whirlwind of a morning we went back to Ocotal, Nicaragua, where we spent the afternoon preparing for the evening service. Phillip Tyson and I broke away for a while before the evening service to visit Second Baptist Church, another little church in an even more impoverished part of Ocotal. While there I was able to share my testimony. The people, with stories so different from my own, listened as I told them how I came to know the Lord Jesus Christ and how I wanted to live for him. No matter who or where we are, we all obtain salvation the same way, by putting our faith and trust in Jesus Christ and the finished work of Calvary.

On our way back we crossed a river where a few ladies were washing clothes, which I understand was a common practice there. About 500 attended the evening service in Ocotal in an outdoor walled area. John Nelms preached a message on true religion and did a good, non-offensive job of exposing false religions.

Washing clothes in the river

The next day we visited three more Nicaraguan churches in out of the way places. I was both touched and excited to see faithful little works tucked away all over the countryside. Any kind of stable church under

Bob Tyson's direction, it seemed, also had at least one, if not several, additional mission works. Everywhere we visited by vehicle, these preachers had walked in the past, starting mission works and living off very little. Oh, how they put us in the USA to shame! The exchange rate in Nicaragua at that time was 3,000,800 Cordoba to 1 US dollar. The government actually took the bills and stamped a new value on them almost daily. Life for these poor people is just a matter of survival!

That afternoon I was in a short service with Phillip Tyson and a church member in Ocotal for the express purpose of praying for the church member. The church member died the next morning of a heart attack. He was 38 years old and married with five children. We donated 75 dollars to buy lumber to build a casket. There is no embalming or fussing over the body. The deceased was laid out on a table at home where the family and friends would be up all night mourning over him.

John Nelms preached a good message again that night, and about five or six hundred attended again, but only two trusted Christ for salvation. Phillip shared that the people are so steeped in false religions that it takes time for the truth of the gospel to sink in.

By this time, I had ridden many miles over rough roads in the back of a pickup truck, and it was wearing on me, but I was so glad I had come. It was fairly common to see a lone soldier or several soldiers along the road with AK-47s, which was always a reminder of the uneasy political situation. Traveling the roads in Honduras and Nicaragua, we met with many surprises and hazardous situations, but the Lord spared us each time. Often on a two-lane road a driver would stop and block one lane if he had trouble or if he just wanted to stop for any reason. One time we were directly behind a bus that appeared to be passing the vehicle ahead, so we stayed behind him, only to have the bus pull into the left lane and stop abruptly, forcing us to swerve around him. On another occasion we rounded a curve to find a herd of cattle in the road. Yet another time we passed what we assumed to be a father and son on foot pulling an oxcart full of firewood down the road. At these times, if a driver had been coming from the other direction, we could not have avoided colliding with whatever was obstructing the road or the oncoming vehicle. God most certainly protected us constantly as we served him there in those countries.

A saying in Honduras: "Life is hard and then you die."

On Sunday we went to Samoto, Nicaragua, to hold services in a rented theater building. The people there wanted the Tysons to start a Christian school and already had over 400 students signed up. The locals didn't have the resources to start the school, but still felt compelled to do something.

On the following day we went to Condega, Nicaragua, to start three days of meetings in churches in the surrounding areas. While there, we stayed in a place where the Tysons had lived for ten years. Although they still own the property in Condega, the Tysons had to leave when the Sandinistas took power. The Sandinistas, led by Daniel Ortega, is a communist rebel army which toppled the Somoza ruling family in 1979 and ruled over the government of Nicaragua from 1979 to 1990. The Sandinistas once attempted an air attack on this building but were shot down by men positioned on the roof. Later they took control of the town and occupied the building. By a miracle of God, the property was eventually returned to the Tysons. The building had been a showplace to God's glory before the war, but now it was run down and badly in need of repairs.

During those three days we visited a number of churches in the Condega area and held services with dear people who love the Lord and serve him faithfully. At one church the people waited over two hours for us to arrive. People generally walk a great distance any day or any time of day to gather in their Sunday best to worship and fellowship. These people are not tightly bound by time and schedule, and they serve God at great sacrifice. Many of these people have remained faithful to God at the threat of their lives. I stood in awe of their love and dedication and how they made do with what they had and yet honored God with their meager incomes.

At Smerna Baptist Church, a small church in the interior, way up in the mountains in an area called Portillo, I had the privilege of sharing my testimony. Pastor Santos from Condega was used by the Lord to help start this church six years earlier in the middle of the war. He used to walk three hours into this area to minister to these people. The church is now thriving with 120 members and has its own pastor. The people had originally built a mud building to worship in, but they were dissatisfied with its appearance and wanted to build something better with which to serve the Lord. The current church building was built by the nationals with no outside money. Only the cement was purchased; everything else, even the bricks, had all been made by hand. These people walked one to two miles to get to services and had already established another mission work. They take their faith very seriously and are deeply committed to the Great Commission.

At Mount Horeb Baptist Church, located in the mountains outside of Condega, we met for worship on the porch of the home of a Christian family. A pig, a chicken and her little chicks, and a dog enjoyed the service with us. I was amazed at how clean the people kept themselves, considering the conditions under which they live. On the way back to Condega, we stopped in Nuevo Pueblo and picked up some people. We ended up with 12 in the back of the pickup, one fellow half in and half out—not exactly a real safe operation, but the people were used to it.

We went back to San Marcos the next day, where I tried to get some rest in preparation for my return trip home. It had been a blessed trip, but once again, I was eager to be homeward bound. The drive to the Tegucigalpa airport was uneventful, *praise the Lord!* Several soldiers with M-16's were stationed at a bridge, but we crossed without incident.

Honduran soldiers with M-16's

Arriving safely at the Tegucigalpa airport, we saw more soldiers also armed with M-16's stationed at the runway. We said our goodbyes, and I boarded the airplane heading for Houston; when I cleared customs, I then flew on to Denver and to Minneapolis, and drove three hours to Park Rapids. Home at last!

The Tysons were doing fantastic work there in Honduras and Nicaragua. They sought to meet people's physical needs, thus opening the doors to meet the spiritual. I met a number of young people on this trip who had accepted Christ as their Savior and were mentored under the Tysons. These young people are now pastors, pastors' wives, and church members used by God in many wonderful ways. Since that trip, Bob and Joan have gone home to be with the Lord. Stephany, that four-month-old, grew up and got married, and now she, along with her husband, her dad Phillip, and her uncle Steve head up the Good Samaritan Ministries.

15

Mission Field Hardships

"Thou therefore endure hardness, as a good soldier of Jesus Christ."
—*2 Timothy 2:3*

Early April of 1991 we flew the Piper Aztec to International Falls, Minnesota, and took Pastor Bob Crane of First Baptist Church on a mission trip along with some members of his church, Burnie Eckland, Julie MacDougall, and Mary Wrucke, who at the time was 79 years old. Our destination was Guerrero, Chihuahua, Mexico, to work with Jerry and Marti Collins, who were sent out by First Baptist Church of Milford, Ohio. We stopped overnight at the Bearing Precious Seed Ministry in El Paso, Texas, with Carlos Demarest, where Warren and Joanne Klenk were now serving the Lord. We arrived early enough in the afternoon to allow Warren the opportunity to take us across the border to Juarez, Mexico, where he was assisting a church that had been established at the city dump.

By this time in the Wings ministry, I had seen people living in very humble circumstances, but if I had not actually seen these dwellings and how the people lived, or more accurately speaking, existed, under these conditions, I would have had a hard time believing its reality. The sight was beyond description! The people had built shanties out of whatever they could salvage from the garbage. They also salvaged food and clothing, and on cool nights they burned discarded, worn out tires in an attempt to stay warm. The stench was overwhelming to someone not used to it. Humanly speaking, these unfortunate people had little or no hope, but Christ loved them and died for their precious souls.

We returned to El Paso and went to the Golden Corral restaurant for our evening meal, feeling so blessed of God to have been born in the USA under a form of government ordained of God. We also were feeling somewhat guilty for the abundance we enjoyed, when so much of the world has so little, especially those just across our southern border. South of our border the inhabitants' forefathers came looking for gold and personal riches, whereas our forefathers came denying themselves and searching for the freedom to worship the living God. That focus makes all the difference!

Warren Klenk at city dump church with some church people

We spent the night at the Bearing Precious Seed base in El Paso. The next morning, we headed to the airport for our departure to Guerrero. We were airborne about 10:30 a.m. for our five-minute flight to Juarez, where we landed to clear Mexican customs. All went well, and Mexican customs was no more than several visits from office to office, paying the usual fees. Airborne again, we had a rough ride with strong crosswinds for about two hours all the way to Guerrero, and these conditions taxed the Aztec's performance capabilities to the limit. The Guerrero airstrip was located on a bluff with a pretty good drop off at the north end of the strip. On our approach for landing toward the south we got into a downdraft that took us below the runway elevation, and after applying full power, I began to think we might have to land on a road or field short of the runway. I asked the Lord to intervene, and at that moment we began to climb back to a normal approach profile, and we made a normal safe landing!

"Call unto me, and I will answer thee........" Jeremiah 33:3. He graciously answered my call! In 38 years of flying to this point, I had experienced several emergencies, but never an accident. *Only God!*

Rex Cobb was also a missionary in the Guerrero area, where I attended church the night of our arrival, and was able to give a 15-minute testimony and message. The next day Pastor Collins took us to the Tarahumara Indians in Copper Canyon, which is much like our Grand Canyon, located at Creel, Chihuahua.

On the way we stopped to visit and encourage a national pastor, Alfanzo Sanchez, and his family. A couple of years earlier Alfanzo had been beaten and his wife raped, but in spite of the attack and heartache, they overcame the trauma and remained faithful. They are missionaries to the Tarahumara, a very fierce and isolated people who have become known in more recent years for their phenomenal physical endurance and ability to run long distances in Mexico's extremely hot, dry conditions. Their culture is given to idolatry and debauchery. Some of them still live in caves and cliff dwellings. What a sight that was! They are certainly a people that desperately need Christ, and some have been gloriously saved!

Cave home (above) and Tarahumara woman at home entrance

We returned to Guerrero that evening, and the next morning I took Jerry Collins on a survey flight with Pastor Crane with Burnie Ecklund riding along. We were up for about an hour looking for other remote villages in the area, as well as the roads to get there, so that Jerry could get to those villages and preach the gospel. We found and made note of several other villages and roads before returning to Guerrero.

After lunch we drove to a nearby village to check out the possibility of having a service there that night. We were supposed to have a projector with us but failed to obtain it. So we decided that without the film, it would be hard to get the people out. So we went to the nearby village of La Junta in the afternoon and went door to door handing out tracts and booklets of the gospels of John and Romans. We went to another village where they had an established work and held a service there that night after canvassing the villagers. Pastor Crane preached to a small crowd and though no one, as far as we know, trusted Christ, the seed was sown.

It was a blessed and heart transforming week! At the close of our time in Guerrero, we prayed together, said our goodbyes, and took to the air at 8:00 a.m. We flew to Juarez, cleared Mexican customs in about 45 minutes, and arrived in El Paso midmorning. We cleared US customs, refueled, filed an IFR flight plan, and took to the air again, headed for home, arriving back in Park Rapids later that evening. Another mission trip, by God's grace, was safely completed.

A short time after that trip I received the following letter from Warren Klenk:

> Perhaps you will remember our trips to Guererro in the state of Chihuahua, Mexico, earlier this spring. You made the Wings airplane available to missionary Jerry Collins and to several of us from Bearing Precious Seed for a survey flight in the area. On that flight we saw some villages that we had never seen before and would not have known about had we not been able to see them from the air. I would like to share with you some of the results of that very well-spent hour. Two weeks after the survey flight we visited the town of Preson de Golondrinas. You might remember that town because of the large lagoon nearby. The people were very friendly as we visited door to door, and many came out for the gospel film and preaching. At the invitation 96 people stepped forward to trust Jesus Christ as their personal Savior. About three weeks later we visited the ranches of Tres Ojitos (Three Little Eyes) and Nuaherachic. Not appearing on any map, they are about five miles off the main highway on a very rough and dusty road near the city of Madera. On those two nights 135 people responded to the gospel for salvation. Because of the Wings airplane and your time, 231 people are saved today and going to heaven instead of hell. The airplane is still a great and effective tool for searching out the lost and reaching them for Christ. I am sure that all of those who support Wings As Eagles through their sacrificial giving will be encouraged and recognize that they had a definite part in the salvation of many souls. Many times your name and ministry have been brought before the Lord in prayer. May God richly bless you!

A letter like this is such a great encouragement! If this were the only report of this nature, it would make the Wings ministry worth every prayer, every sacrifice, every effort, and every dollar that it has taken to make it a reality!

Another memorable trip in the Aztec took place later that April. A few months earlier, Juanita and I had been on a driving trip to Prince Albert, Saskatchewan, Canada. It was recommended that we pay a visit to Pastor Ken Shaffer at New Testament Baptist Church in Larimore, North Dakota, on the way. We had a great visit with Pastor Shaffer and encouraged him to take a mission trip with us. He was a little concerned about the finances needed, so I suggested that he take loose change offerings for the mission trip, which he did, and was able to raise the required funds in a relatively short time.

This trip took place April 29 to May 4, 1991, to Monterrey, Mexico. Pastor Shaffer showed up for the trip dressed for warm spring weather, thinking that we were going south to warmer weather, which normally would have been fine; however, after takeoff, the Janitrol heater wouldn't fire up, which meant that we were without heat in the airplane. Our first stop was Denver, where we were to pick up Pastor T. J. Smith from Harvest Baptist Church in Albany, Oregon, to join us. We ran into some fairly heavy rain in the area of Sioux Falls and Huron, South Dakota, and in order to stay out of some of the bad weather, I climbed to 12,000 feet on an IFR flight plan and broke out on top into smooth air. Of course, the temperature was much colder at that altitude, and we were all getting uncomfortably cold, but Pastor Shaffer was getting *really* cold. We had a blanket on board and gave it to him, which of course was a big help, but it was still cold enough that Juanita had frost in her shoes before we arrived in Denver, where it was much warmer. It warmed up from there as we headed south to Laredo, Texas, where we spent the night at Rio Grande Missionary Help, with Bill Waldrop.

The next morning Bill Waldrop took us out to breakfast and then across the border to Nuevo Laredo to see a work that he was pastoring. Bill had us back to the Laredo airport and we flew on to Monterrey, Mexico, arriving later that morning. We waited there for missionary Doyle Johnson to pick us up and take us to the village of San Juanito, east of Monterrey, for an open-air service that evening.

Doyle Johnson and family

The next day we went to see Cascada Cola de Caballo, Horse Tail Falls, a beautiful waterfall just a few miles away. After lunch with missionary Tommy Ashcraft, who lived and ministered nearby, we went to the Juvenile Detention Center. There Martin Malacada, a Mexican national, preached, and a number of young boys raised their hands to receive Christ as their Savior.

On Sunday Pastor Shaffer and Pastor Smith preached and I sang a solo at each morning and evening service at the Monte Hebron Bible Institute. We all kept busy preaching or serving in other ways, with souls coming to Christ at every service. It was, as always, a great blessing to all our hearts to see God so at work in the lives of the listeners. The eyes of our group were opened to the spiritual poverty, as well as the great material needs, south of our border.

Before departing for home, we purchased Mexican blankets to keep us warm on the way. The weather was bad in Denver on our return, and we were forced to land and stay overnight in Pueblo, Colorado. The next morning the weather was beautiful. We flew to Denver, dropped off Pastor Smith to catch his flight home to Oregon, then proceeded on to Grand Forks, North Dakota, with Pastor Shaffer. When he disembarked, he commented as he folded his blanket, "These trips aren't for wimps, are they?!"

Pastor Shaffer has been a friend and pastor of a supporting church since that day. I must admit that most of these trips are not for wimps. I could have canceled the trip because of the inoperative heater, but I didn't believe it was what God wanted. I am so glad I just stayed focused on the ministry rather than on our comfort!

16

Road Trip

"And whatsoever ye do, do it heartily, as to the Lord, and not unto men . . . for ye serve the Lord Christ."—Colossians 3:23–24

Dennis Deneau and his family were so kind and patient with us! Since they were often on the road for the Bearing Precious Seed Ministry, they allowed us to move out of the travel trailer we had parked at their place after we sold the resort and into their home while they were gone. The Deneaus' would eventually relocate to Michigan and continue traveling for the Bearing Precious Seed ministry from there, but for that time, it was such a great blessing to have a house.

The spring of 1991 we still did not have a clear direction for a move, so we began to look for a cottage on a lake in the area and found a small, suitable place on Fifth Crow Wing Lake about eight miles east of Park Rapids. We made an offer but could not move forward on it at that time, because we had to travel to Pontiac, Michigan, for a propeller overhaul for the Aztec. The realtor told us that if we didn't do something right then, the cottage would be gone by the time we returned. I told him that if that was the place God wanted us to have, it would still be available when we got back. Upon our return it was still available, and we made the purchase and moved in. It was a blessing to have our own place again, though we still believed a move for the ministry was imminent. In the meantime, we were happy in our little cottage and, as always, enjoyed the lake and a beautiful view.

In May, just a few months after our trip to Honduras, the Tysons asked me to help drive two well-used school buses and a pickup truck from Villa Rica, Georgia, to San Marcos, Honduras. I accepted the invitation and on August 15 left for Villa Rica, just outside of Atlanta. I drove from Park Rapids to Minneapolis and stayed with Juanita's mother, and early the next morning I flew out on Continental Airlines to Atlanta. Tyson's oldest son Phillip, who was 21, was heading up the trip to San Marcos, and was waiting for me at the gate. We stopped at a music store to pick up a couple of large speakers for their sound system in Honduras and arrived at their home and office in Villa Rica about 6:30 p.m.

I had had a head cold when I left home, and it was getting worse. I tried to lie down as I was not feeling well but sleep evaded me for the most part. Preparation on the two buses continued, and there was a lot of last minute rush and confusion. The driving crew of four (Phillip, his brother Steve, one other man, and me) finally left Villa Rica at 12:30 a.m. We stopped at a nearby gas station for fuel and air for the tires. Upon airing up the tires of the '69 Ford bus, we discovered the inside dual on the right was flat and had swallowed the valve stem. We nursed it 26 miles down the road to a truck stop, where we were able to get a new tire and continue on our way. We drove around the clock, at speeds of 30 to 45 miles an hour most of the time, and everything ran fairly smoothly the first night and following day.

On the second night, Steve Tyson, Phillip's 17-year-old brother, and I were driving the Nissan pickup, and I let Steve do the driving while I slept. I was awakened suddenly by a violent vibration. Steve had fallen asleep and ran into a guard rail. The right tires had climbed the guard rail and were bouncing off the posts, threatening to roll the vehicle. Startled and now wide awake, I grabbed the wheel and steered us into the roll and back onto the road. Fortunately, nothing was hurt, and though Steve felt bad and his confidence was shaken, the Lord was merciful and took care of us. Except for God's miraculous hand of protection, this incident could have been disastrous. Phillip saw the whole thing happen, as he was following us in one of the buses. He hollered at us on the CB to pull over. After a short talk I took over the driving, and we continued, praising God for his protection and care! We continued to Matamoros, Mexico, where we stopped to clear customs.

One of the buses was filled with clothing and the other was filled with bicycles intended for the national preachers and families in Honduras and Nicaragua. After much delay, we were not allowed to enter Mexico with the clothing; the Mexican authorities were apparently afraid that we would sell the clothing in their country. We had to turn around and return to Brownsville, Texas to drop off the clothing at a local church. After completing that task, we proceeded back across the border and joined our team once again. After completing all the paperwork and paying customs fees, we were back on the road, though now many hours later. The authorities didn't seem too concerned about the bicycles; however, a Mexican agent was placed on one of our buses being required to accompany us all the way to the Guatemalan border.

All rolled along well until we arrived in Tampico, Mexico, and stopped for fuel about midnight. We were approached by the police and offered an escort through the city. Phillip told them that would not be necessary. He was promptly told that they were going to give us an escort through the city—no choice—and that it would cost us 50 dollars. After getting the escort and paying the 50 dollars, we thought it through and realized that they had probably done us a favor. Without the escort, only God himself knows how many times we could have been stopped by other police and how much money we might have had to pay to get through the city and be on our way.

We drove steadily through the night. Arriving in Veracruz, we stopped to see the Don Rogers family for a brief visit, then continued our trip south to pick up the Pan American highway. Things were still going smoothly, but we were all getting pretty worn out! We all needed to spend a night in a hotel somewhere to get some decent rest. The next day as we were driving through the state of Chiapas, in southern Mexico, one of our guys became very ill and began running a high fever. We decided to find a hospital in the next larger city. Then we came across a medical mission station in the middle of nowhere, just off the highway, so we stopped there for help. A missionary doctor took our guy in, gave him a shot, and in five minutes he felt much better. The fever had broken! I could not believe it, but the evidence was obvious, and he continued to feel better from that point on. I don't know what was in that shot, but whatever it was, it worked! God again performed a miracle, and it reminded me again of the verse in Isaiah 65:24 which says, *"And it shall come to pass, that before they call, I will answer; and while they are yet speaking, I will hear."*

At the Guatemalan border we had to give away a couple of bicycles to border agents in order to get through customs. Our Mexican agent left us at that point, and we took on a Guatemalan agent to accompany us through the country. Somewhere about halfway through Guatemala, a group of soldiers stopped us and asked for money. Phillip got us on our way again for one dollar. God is so good!

Looking back, I stand amazed that we survived the narrow, winding roads through the mountains of Guatemala at night! I was driving one of the buses and fighting to stay awake, especially as I drove into the morning sunrise. All I can say is that God was certainly watching over us throughout that trip.

Reaching the border of El Salvador, we had to go through the same painstaking customs process. Again, we had to leave behind a couple bicycles, our Guatemalan agent left us, and we took on an El Salvadorian agent to ride with us through El Salvador. Upon reaching the outskirts of San Salvador late at night, we were warned that guerrilla warfare was going on in the area, and we needed to hold up somewhere. We pulled into a closed Texaco station about 11:00 p.m. and slept on the bus until morning, awakened every now and then by distant gunfire. That had a way of getting our attention!

It rained during the night, and as we departed the city and I was driving the bus once again, I turned a corner where several people were waiting for the city bus. I hit a fairly large mud puddle, splashing up a wave of water and drenching a well-dressed lady. I felt horrible, but there was nothing I could do, and stopping was out of the question. I still remember that moment, and I'm sure she has never forgotten it either!

We made it through El Salvador and arrived at the Honduran border, our trip almost over. We lost our agent, and Phillip spent several hours going from office to office, taking care of all kinds of paperwork, paying fees and making both buses and the pickup truck legal in Honduras. We arrived in San Marcos de Colon late in the evening, worn out but safe, and all vehicles in one piece. We had been on the road for seven full days. God had protected us and shown us his mercy every mile. It was an experience of a lifetime, and certainly one I would never forget. A couple of days later I caught a Continental flight from the airport in Tegucigalpa and was on my way home. Home is such a wonderful place to be after a trip like that, or any trip for that matter. However, the joy of knowing you are serving the Lord and are in his perfect will is even more wonderful.

17

Never Quit

"And let us not be weary in well doing: for in due season we shall reap. ......"—Galatians 6:9

On one of our visits to see Gary and his family in Denver, Colorado, Gary's pastor, Craig Scott, invited us to move back to Denver and base the Wings As Eagles ministry out of Woodside Baptist Church. We felt kind of isolated in the small town of Park Rapids and had continued to seek the Lord's direction concerning a move even after we had settled into the cottage. The Lord laid it on our hearts at that time to accept that offer, and we moved back to the Denver area in the spring of 1992.

One of the big advantages of being back in Denver was Gary's availability to help with aircraft maintenance, since he was licensed and I was not. Gary flew a number of mission trips with me, and he was certainly God's man for the hour in keeping the airplane maintained. The move back to Denver, we have no doubt, was the perfect will of God for us at that time. Pastor Scott became a dear pastor to us and Woodside Baptist Church a supportive church family; in fact, Woodside became our largest contributor and remains so to this day, with Pastor Scott also later becoming one of our advisory board members.

We flew several mission trips out of Woodside, with Pastor Scott on board at least once, despite his tendency to get airsick. On that trip he handled his distress so quietly and discreetly that I didn't know he had a problem until after we landed. That was his first mission trip out of the country, and God used it in his life in a wonderful way, moving in his heart to take many more mission trips since that day, preaching and teaching in countries across the globe. We learned and grew in the Lord in a wonderful way under his ministry, and he remains a great blessing to Wings as Eagles and to us personally.

Gary working on the Aztec

* * * * * * *

In October of 1992 Doug Kalapp and I flew a mission trip to Monterrey, Coahuila, Mexico, landing in Granite City, Illinois, near St. Louis, Missouri, to pick up Pastor Wayne Musatics and some of the men of Central Baptist Church. Once we arrived in Monterrey, we were joined by a national missionary, Martin Malacada, sent out of Tommy Ashcraft's church in Monterrey. Martin loaded the six of us from the Wings As Eagles team into his older maxi van, along with six Mexican nationals, and the twelve of us headed for the village of Dulces Nombres in Nuevo Leon, a lumber mill village at the end of the trail on top of a small mountain.

The trip went well for the first 50 miles or so until, to reach our destination, we were forced to leave the main road and take a trail through the wilderness and farmers' pastures. At one point we had to drive across a shallow river, where we got high centered on a rock in the middle of the river. A number of us got out, myself included, and we tried pushing the van to no avail. There was a farm close by, and the farmer came with a tractor to retrieve us from the river. Soon we were on our way again down the trails. How Martin knew where he was going, I will never know!

We finally arrived at a slightly better-established road and a meeting shack, where a flatbed truck carrying food supplies was to come by on which we all could ride to the lumber village at the end of the road. What we thought would be a two-hour ride on the flat bed turned out to be a six-hour ride at a snail's pace up a steep mountain. Often our outside dual wheel was no more than six inches from the cliff's edge, with a thousand-foot drop to the canyon valley floor below. At times we wondered what we were doing there, but it wasn't long until we knew.

Finally arriving at Dulces Nombres, we found 80 to 90 people living in little wood-framed shacks, with dirt floors, no electricity, and no running water. An old church building that had been used by a Presbyterian group back in the 1930s and abandoned in 1940 was the only sign of any Christian influence in the settlement. Apparently, there had not been any gospel outreach to that village since that time, and no one in the village possessed a Bible that we knew of.

We settled into a bunk house that night that had wooden floors and two bedrooms with a short hallway between them. Pastor Musatics and I slept in our sleeping bags on an old double bed spring. Doug Kalapp and one of the other men slept in the other room under similar conditions, and one of our team slept on the hallway floor. Sometime in the night our man on the floor was awakened by rats crawling on him. None of us slept very well.

The next morning, we fixed breakfast in a cooking shack with an open fire pit. Breakfast actually turned out pretty good! We then split up into six teams of two and went door to door sharing the gospel and giving out gospel literature. That evening we held a service outdoors in the cool mountain air. Many people came and sat on the rocks in the dark to hear the preaching. A total of 55 people, young and old, received Jesus Christ as their Lord and Savior that night!

Breakfast being prepared

The next day we talked to our truck driver about a ride back down the mountain, and at first he refused, because he had a full load of lumber going back down, but, understanding that there was no other transportation for us, he relented and let us ride the seven-hour trip on top of the lumber. It was a drizzly day, and though we had a tarp, it was hard to stay dry, but our hearts were filled with joy as we made our way back down the mountain, rejoicing over those who had trusted Christ.

We arrived safely back at our van and headed back down the pasture trail. The lumber truck was going in the same direction, and he headed out in front, with us trailing behind. The rain had softened the ground, so we made it only a short distance before we got stuck in a large mud puddle. The truck driver saw our dilemma and stopped to help us. He backed up, hooked onto us with a rope, and pulled us all the way down the trail, across the river, and up to the main dirt road. There was a little island in the road with puddles on both sides, and he chose the right side, next to a fence line, and in the middle of the puddle, he sank in up to the rear axle. We unhooked and tried to help, but there wasn't much we could do. A farmer came along with a tractor and tried to pull him out, to no avail.

We gave the trucker some money for his help, thanked him very sincerely, and loaded up in the van again, hoping to make it through the puddle on the left side of the island. By God's grace, we pushed through, and we were on our way back to Monterrey. I felt so sorry for the trucker. I am sure that he had to unload his lumber in order to get out of that hole. God certainly used him to meet our needs at the time, and we continued down the road, again praising God for his goodness!

Pastor Musatics and his men returned to their homes in the St. Louis, Missouri, area, grateful for the blessings God had bestowed on them in the USA, but also burdened to do more to get the gospel to their lost and dying countrymen and to the world while there is still time. God says in Lamentations 3:51, *"Mine eye affecteth mine heart ...."*

* * * * * * *

Shortly after our move back to Denver we were put in contact with recently retired US Air Force Major, Harry Winters. He and his family loved the Lord, and Harry had a commercial pilot's certificate, a flight instructor's rating, and about 500 hours of flight time. Harry was looking for an aviation ministry where he could serve the Lord. Juanita and I flew on Continental Airlines to Austin, Texas, where the Winters were living at the time, to meet Harry, his wife Deloris (Cookie), and their children.

Harry Winters and family shortly after joining Wings

We quickly realized that we were on the same page doctrinally and in terms of vision for ministry, so we invited them to become a part of the Wings ministry. Shortly thereafter, Harry and his family moved to Denver and joined Woodside Baptist Church and Wings As Eagles.

Harry Winters began flying with me on almost all our mission trips to gain experience and prepare to occasionally take full responsibility for future mission trips. On one of our trips together with a Woodside Baptist group, we flew to Monterrey, Mexico, to work with Missionary Tommy Ashcraft. Along with taking the gospel door to door, our project was to build trusses and a roof for a second story on their church building. One evening after our meal I began to share a little about starting the Wings ministry and some of the trials and opposition I had experienced at the outset.

"I was tempted to quit at least a thousand times," I told the group.

One of the men on the trip, Paul Davis, a contractor who was spearheading the roof project, reached over, patted me on the back, and said, "Thank you, Bob, for not quitting, because if you had, we wouldn't be here tonight!"

That pat on the back and statement was used by God to encourage my heart and made me more determined than ever before to never quit, unless God made it abundantly clear that he was changing our life's direction. At the time of the writing of this book, we are in our thirty-sixth year of Wings ministry, and God continues to greatly bless!

Harry Winters also served as the Wings' treasurer, and within a couple years I felt confident to send him on mission trips without me, which made it possible for Juanita and me to present the ministry in other churches while he was gone. Harry and his dear wife Cookie and family were, and remain, a great blessing and asset to the Wings ministry.

In 1993 Mark Robertson, a missionary who was serving the Lord in Uranium City, Saskatchewan, Canada, contacted us because he needed help undertaking a construction project to add a large room to his home and church building in order for them to meet under one roof for worship and Sunday school services. I was sure God would provide a crew and we would do our best to bring him the help he needed.

We put together a crew from Woodside Baptist Church and took to the air for Uranium City on August 9, 1993. A contractor from California by the name of Rich Young, with whom Mark was already well acquainted, flew in on a commercial airline to head up the project. Rich was a strong, driven, get-it-done type of guy, and in the ten working days that we were there, the project was completed. Working with Rich Young was a tremendous experience to say the least! He loved the Lord, giving of himself for the Lord's service whenever and wherever God enabled.

Adding on to the Robertson home for church services

Uranium City is a very unusual place and certainly in need of a gospel out-reach. The village is very isolated, with no road access except for a winter road across Lake Athabasca in months when the lake is solidly frozen. Similar to many other places in northern Canada, the only other way in or out is by air or boat. Once a thriving uranium mining town with a population of about 5000, Uranium City had a beautiful new school, city hall, hospital, recreational facilities, and a lot of construction going on, when the uranium mine shut down around 1981.

The town's population dropped to about 500 almost overnight, and Uranium City soon dwindled to a ghost town after that. When we were there on our first trip in 1993, the population was about 250, mostly Chipewyan Dene natives; and at this writing that population has dropped again to about 80.

With so many vacant and unused buildings, the whole town basically became a hardware store and lumber yard for the taking. If we needed lumber for a project, we just bought a vacant home for 10 or 15 dollars and tore it down for the materials. Vandalism was rampant amongst the physical buildings, and broken lives were common in many of the people left behind, with alcoholism, drug abuse, and immorality taking their toll. The extremely cold temperatures in the region caused potholes in the roads, heaving and buckling of floors in the unheated and abandoned buildings, and other issues related to a harsh climate.

Wings as Eagles continues to serve with Jim at Beacon Baptist Church and Bible Camp every summer by flying into remote villages and transporting the native young people to Beacon Bible Camp and then home again. While there at the camp, of course, the Wings team functions in any way they may be needed, serving as counsellors, kitchen staff, game directors, and preachers; doing building repairs and maintenance, salvage, and cleaning; transporting groceries, other supplies, and other camp staff to the campgrounds.

Beacon Bible Camp chapel

A couple of years later, in 1996, Mark Robertson left Uranium City to plant a church in Yellowknife, Northwest Territories. Jim Pfaffenroth, a former airline pilot, had taken mission trips to Uranium City through Bob Jones University and had established the unique ministry of Beacon Bible Camp, a fly-in summer camp that brings together children from the remote villages in the area, often from abusive and dysfunctional homes, for at least a week of Bible preaching, games, and gospel outreach. God gave Jim Pfaffenroth and his family a burden for the town and area, so when Brother Robertson moved, he took the ministry and still proclaims the gospel there today, the only gospel preacher anywhere in the area.

Beacon Bible Camp kitchen and dining hall

The following is part of a letter I received from Jim Pfaffenroth in May of 2000:

> Once again you overwhelmed us with your love and generosity. I feel like I have been filled and then filled again with the blessings of our Lord. To say thank you seems so small and yet I can't express my gratitude in the right way to you and the team for all that was done for us. The house looks absolutely beautiful. Thank you. Sharon and I love the floor that you put in the kitchen. It made everything bright and beautiful. Thank you for that blessing. I trust that as a result of your hard work on our

home that many would be influenced to "taste and see that the Lord is good." Thank you for making the flights to Fort McMurray for the Bible Camp. That indeed was a big help to us. I was humbled again by your generosity. Our financial needs have been great, and your love gift was an answer to prayer. May God bless you for your sensitivity to our needs.

After our time together in Uranium City, Rich Young asked to join Wings As Eagles and made himself available for any future construction mission trips that the Lord would lead us to participate in. Rich and his dear wife Carolyn became another great addition and blessing to the Wings ministry. He has been on many construction mission trips since then and continues to serve to this day as an advisor, though he is now 85 years of age.

Rich and Carolyn Young

A few years ago we came very close to losing Rich on a trip to Laredo, Texas. We were working on a project with Bill Waldrop and the Rio Grande Missionary Helps ministry. He was experiencing a heart attack, and as we rushed him to the hospital, he was in a rare sense of humor and promised me that should he die, he wanted me to have his toothbrush! I thanked him and assured him that I was deeply grateful for his generosity and thoughtfulness. Rich had a rough time, but he survived, and with his sense of humor intact.

The year 1994 was a tremendously busy and blessed time for the Wings As Eagles ministry, as well as for each of us personally. God's grace enabled us to take eleven mission trips to the fields of Canada, Mexico, Dominican Republic, Turks and Caicos Islands, Guatemala, and Granada. Thousands of Scripture portions were distributed throughout the year, and many hundreds of souls came to know the Lord Jesus Christ as Savior.

One mission trip was to missionary Don Rogers in Veracruz, Mexico, who had contacted Wings asking for help with an ongoing building project. Harry Winters had flown several mission trips as the captain by this time, and we sent him out as the captain on this trip. Afterward Harry wrote the following:

In December we flew a trip from Woodside Baptist Church to Veracruz, Mexico, to help Don Rogers in laying concrete blocks for the church building he and his church are constructing. Paul Davis, Rich Young, and our youth pastor Ed Boontjer from Woodside, as on previous construction trips, provided indispensable construction expertise in laying the block. Don Rogers referred to the Wings team as "Wings of Cherubim" working with him on this project. As usual, there was much opposition from Satan. On Wednesday night during church services, there was a procession from the local Catholic Church parading a life-size statue of the Virgin Mary past the church with such a tremendous din and tumult that our services were totally disrupted for a short time. This incident was a graphic illustration of the opposition and challenges which face us as we go about to serve Christ in his great commission, preaching the gospel to every creature.

I cannot thank God enough for those of you who pray and share to make this ministry possible. My family and I count it a great privilege to be a part of this ministry, and we are excited about the tremendous potential for Wings in the days ahead.

Missionary Don Rogers wrote the following:
The month of November found us working hard to finish pouring all the floors on the downstairs building and tearing down an old cement storage room. Everyone helped, including the women and children. Our little cement mixer that we bought last

year, which holds a half bag of cement plus gravel and sand, was really groaning at the gears—and so were we!! But thank the Lord, we finished just in time to receive the six-man work crew from Wings As Eagles the first week of December. To us, they were Wings of Cherubim sent from God! They worked fast and furiously and laid two thousand blocks in four and a half days. They had such sweet attitudes about them; how our hearts were touched as they gave testimonies at our Wednesday night service, thanking the Lord for the privilege of being able to come and work as unto the Lord. We know that some of these men took precious vacation time and spent their hard-earned money to be able to come down here; they came from freezing temperatures to work in an unusually warm spell that we had that week. But they had the true spirit of giving that will be engraved in our hearts forever, and they certainly prepared our hearts for the real Christmas message, *"For God so loved the world, that he gave "*

* * * * * * *

Pastor Luther Goff pastored a church in Regina, Saskatchewan, Canada, and allowed me to present the Wings ministry in his church. Sometime later he was with me on a mission trip in the Piper Aztec to Guerrero, Chihuahua, Mexico, where we served with missionaries Jerry and Marti Collins. While there, we decided to go visit a work in Ejido Constitucion, a small village about 140 miles south of El Paso, Texas, a ministry we had visited a couple of times before with Carlos Demarest. Jerry told me there was a grass strip there, on the south side of the village, so we made plans to fly over. It was a rather short flight, so I took my passengers and flew there while Jerry and his wife Marti drove. Upon arrival, sure enough, there was the grass strip, and we made our landing safely.

Shortly after our landing, a man came over to check us out, but he was drunk, and we realized we could not leave the parked aircraft unattended, so we decided to tow the airplane through the village to the church and park it there, where it would be safe and we could keep an eye on it. We had a preaching service and enjoyed our fellowship with the people that night.

The next morning when I calculated our departure from the grass strip, I realized that with the load I had, the field elevation, and the fact that the village dump was at the end of the strip, there was no way we could use the grass strip for takeoff. Instead I decided to use the paved highway that had a nice, long, straight stretch with no obstructions except a road sign, but I thought I could be airborne before getting to it.

We towed the airplane through the village onto the highway with Pastor Goff in the copilot seat next to me. One of our passengers was a little concerned. I told him if he were a believer in the Lord Jesus Christ, there was nothing to worry about; he was in the Lord's hands no matter what. I'm not sure if that helped him or not!

We sent Jerry Collins ahead of us a mile or so down the highway to block any traffic; I applied takeoff power, and all was going well until we approached the road sign and we were not yet off the ground. I veered to the right a little to miss the sign with my left wing, and the right wing got into tall weeds—no big problem. We veered back to the center of the highway, and in a short time we were airborne, climbing up between power lines and telephone wires on both sides. Once safely above them, I made a right turn and headed for El Paso. Looking over at Pastor Goff, I commented, "I don't think that I will do that again."

After that eventful trip to Guerrero, God gave Pastor Goff the following poem which he later shared with me:

With Wings As Eagles Mission Air Service

With Wings As Eagles lifting you,
A heavenly perspective comes to view;
And on the horizon of possibility
You may witness what God can see.

Souls in danger, and their dreadful plight
As they wander in the darkness of eternal night,
Subverted by Satan day after day,
Groping in blindness, not knowing the way.

With Wings As Eagles one can go,
And see what God and missionaries know;
People in personal poverty on every hand,
And spiritual drought throughout the land.

Captain Bob Warinner

Hungry children, starving for love,
Wondering if there is really a God above;
They, with dirty hands, and feet, and face,
Are in desperate need of God's saving grace.

With Wings As Eagles one can see,
Sights not common to you and me.
Children taking meals we'd never eat,
Like a dried-up orange peel from off the street.

Others wear clothes we'd use as rags.
Or put on the curb in garbage bags.
Only to look once into their empty eyes,
Will bring from within sobs and sighs.

With Wings As Eagles lives can be changed,
But first, priorities must be rearranged.
If seeing is believing, then we must see,
And let God make a difference, through you and me.

What can be done by us today?
We can give from our hearts and passionately pray.
We could go, bearing precious seed,
To plant and plead with souls in need.

With Wings As Eagles let us rise,
And take our flight to foreign skies.
Let us catch the vision of our coming King,
And labor for souls until we hear the trumpet sing.

Rewards in glory one day will be;
For those who live now, for eternity.
Remember our redemption draweth nigh,
So, lay up treasures in Heaven on high.

With Wings As Eagles, one day we shall stand
Before the God of Glory with books in hand;
I pray all will hear, from the Just and Righteous One,
"Thou good and faithful servant, WELL DONE!"
       —Luther Goff

18

Mercy Flight

". . . let us do good unto all men, especially unto them who are of the household of faith."—Galatians 6:10

In 1993 we had begun to pray seriously and ask the Lord to provide a larger aircraft for the ministry, and the response and support of God's people was incredibly humbling and overwhelming. Within two months God had blessed us with $28,000. Our goal was $100,000, and the airplane God had laid upon our hearts to replace the Piper Aztec was a ten-passenger Piper Navajo Chieftain. By early fall of 1994 God had gloriously blessed, and the goal had been reached. We began to search for the aircraft God would have for this ministry. Between the resources raised and the sale of the Aztec, we had about $150,000 for the purchase of a Piper Chieftain.

The Lord led us to an aircraft in the Detroit, Michigan area. Gary and I flew on Continental Airlines passes to Detroit. The next day we went to see the aircraft, and after giving it the best inspection possible, we flew it on a test flight and made the purchase, flying it home that night in early January 1995. That aircraft has been such a blessing and still serves the Wings ministry today.

Gary and his family moved to Lexington, South Carolina in late spring of 1995 and joined a church there that was very involved in ministries in the Turks and Caicos Islands, especially on the island of Grand Turk. I had flown the Chieftain to Lexington in early January of 1996 and left it with Gary to do the annual inspection for us. On February 10, 1996, I received a call from Gary late in the evening with some bad news. William Randall, one of the missionaries we had worked with on Grand

Turk Islands and the son of Gary's pastor, had been involved in an accident with his motorcycle, his only form of transportation, and was now en route to Miami, Florida on a medevac flight, suffering from an apparent broken neck and severe head injuries. My heart sank. I had been with William just a few weeks before in Columbia, South Carolina. I cried out to the Lord to give the attending doctors wisdom to preserve his life.

William's wife Kathy rode on the medevac with him, leaving their six children ranging in ages from eighteen months to eleven years behind on Grand Turk with another young missionary couple, Steve and Jenna Williamson. It was later discovered that William did not have a broken neck, but a broken collar bone, and, due to severe head injuries, he remained in a coma. He was moved to a hospital in Columbia, South Carolina, where he could be closer to both sets of parents.

We kept in close contact, checking on his progress, and William's father, Pastor Billy Randall, asked us if we would consider flying a mercy trip to the Island to pick up the children and the Williamsons and fly them back to South Carolina. Our answer of course was yes. Gary was just finishing the annual inspection, and the airplane was already positioned for the flight. I caught a Continental flight to Charleston, South Carolina, where Gary and William's father picked me up. Pastor Randall and I left for Grand Turk early the next morning and arrived around 3:30 in the afternoon. Steve Williamson met us at the airport and shared more details of the accident; we even viewed the spot where it had occurred. Grand Turk does not have equipment to handle an emergency of this nature; in fact, had the medevac flight been just thirty minutes later on the day of the accident, William surely would have died.

When I saw the children, my heart broke for them. My mind flooded with the memory of my own father's home going through an airplane accident when I was seven and how I, along with my other siblings, was left to grow up without our father. The Randalls' younger children, of course, could not understand what was going on, while the older ones were confused and concerned for their parents, whom they had not seen for 22 days. Our conversation with them touched on the possibility that the Lord might take their father home, not a comforting thought for little children who love and need their daddy! Three-year-old Joy asked if her daddy was still asleep. We told her that he was, and she said, "When I see him, I am going to kiss him and wake him up!"

That evening Pastor Randall preached at the local Baptist church where the Randalls and the Williamsons had been serving. I was blessed by his message and the obvious faith and peace the Lord had given him. God had given him the grace to trust him for his perfect will for his son. Oh, the sweet peace that only Jesus gives!

The next morning, we loaded everyone into a Dodge van that had been donated to the work some years earlier, and we headed for the airport and our return home. The van was all rusted out; the back of the driver's seat had broken off and was held forward with a two by four; the doors were falling off their hinges; we could see the road through the floorboard; and water had to be put into the radiator at every stop. I could not help reflecting on the fact that so many, many people bask in luxuries in this country, while so often the missionary on the field is left to barely get by. God help us! I believe that we will have to one day give an answer for our hoarding and selfishness and lack of concern for those in need. The aircraft was fueled, the flight plan filed, and all ten of us were on board—something we could not have done with the old Aztec. We took off into the wild blue yonder, headed for Florida and then on to Columbia, South Carolina.

We arrived safely in Columbia later in the afternoon. Kathy had been anxiously awaiting the arrival of her children. With tears in her eyes she waved her arms as we parked. The children got to see their daddy at the hospital that evening, and even though little Joy got to kiss him, he still slept. It was not easy to see William lying there, unresponsive, with a breathing tube in his throat, yet we committed him into the caring hands of the Great Physician who purchased him on the cross of Calvary and who loved him far more than anyone on this planet ever could! God's ways are hard to understand sometimes, but that's where faith comes in: we must trust him!

Eventually William did come out of the coma, but he was never the same again and required much care. Kathy stayed by his side, and though we have not stayed in touch, I understand she faithfully raised her children to love and serve the Lord. We praised God that he had led us to start the Wings As Eagles ministry and blessed us with so many self-sacrificing people to partner with us which make a mercy trip like this one possible. How could we possibly say thank you in an adequate way for the part many have had in helping us serve God in this great ministry.

William Randall, wife Kathy, and their grandchildren in later years

* * * * * *

With Gary in South Carolina and Doug Kalapp getting into churches mostly in the East, our mission trips for the most part were coming together east of the Mississippi. We frequently had to deadhead the airplane, that is, fly without any passengers to our pickup point in the East, which was of course very expensive. I sought God's clear direction as to where he might have us relocate. I prayed for many months, praying the verse found in *Psalm 27:11*, "*Teach me thy way, O LORD, and lead me in a plain path, because of mine enemies.*" The enemy would lead us down a wrong path and destroy this ministry if he could, so we must have a plain path from the Lord!

I finished praying one particular morning in May of 1996 and went on with my day. About three hours later I was out mowing our lawn when my wife called to me and said that I had a phone call, so I stopped the mowing and went in to answer the phone.

"Hello, this is Randy King," said the voice on the other end of the line. "What's this I hear about your wanting to move the ministry back East?"

Pastor Randall King was the pastor of Wyldewood Baptist Church in Oshkosh, Wisconsin. I had been in his church about four years earlier but had not been in contact with him since that time. It took me a short time to figure out who he was. I had included in my prayer request to the Lord that I wanted him to lead us to a church that was debt free, large enough to help us financially if need be, and prepared to adopt and love an aviation ministry.

"Let me tell you a little about our church," Pastor King said, and in our thirty-minute conversation all the points in my prayers were confirmed. Plus, Oshkosh is the aviation capital of the USA!

"We would be honored if you would consider moving the ministry to Wyldewood Baptist Church," Pastor King said. "We want to expand our mission outreach, and we believe that Wings As Eagles would be a great asset to that outreach."

I thanked him for his call and told him I would pray about it. I went back to my mowing, pondering the conversation we had just had. I felt like those who prayed for the Apostle Peter while he was in prison. When their prayer was answered and Peter knocked at their gate, they didn't believe that it was Peter.

Lord, I prayed, *I believe you have just answered my prayer to the letter of every request, and what more is there to pray about? I am going to accept that invitation as your answer and begin to make plans to move to Oshkosh. If that is not where you want us, then you will have to stop us somehow, but if this is your plain path, would you confirm it with a quick sale of our home?*

Juanita and I had been invited to a wedding in Prince Albert, Saskatchewan, Canada, that was to take place about ten days from then, at which I also had been asked to sing. I got back in touch with Pastor King and told him that after the wedding in Canada we would make our way to Oshkosh for a meeting and look around for housing. He said that they had a realtor in the church who could help us.

We contacted a realtor to sell our home in Aurora; I did a little touch up painting and cleaning, and we left for Canada on schedule. While in Canada we received a call from our realtor that our home had sold. Upon arrival in Oshkosh, we met Pastor King and several of the deacons and got together with the realtor in the church, Teresa Schmick. Over the next three days we looked at about forty homes. The first home we looked at was in the small town of Omro, a house that Teresa and her husband Leonard had built and not yet sold, about eight miles west of the church. By the time we were ready to leave for home, we were confused as to what to do, but we kind of liked the home in Omro. In talking with Teresa and her husband Leonard, Leonard offered to discount the price by five thousand dollars if we wanted to purchase it.

"We'll take it!" I told him, so we signed a contract and headed for home.

Our home closing in Aurora was scheduled for July 22, 1996. Upon arriving home, we began to pack and arrange for a U-Haul truck for our move. We needed some help driving our vehicles and found that a couple from Wyldewood Baptist was in Denver for a business meeting. They had flown out from Oshkosh, and the husband would be available to help us while his wife flew back home. Surely, this was just a coincidence, right? We closed the sale on the house on schedule; hit the road for Oshkosh, arriving two days later; and closed on our new home on July 26. When God is in it, things can come together quickly and smoothly! These kinds of happenings in our lives have made God so real to us and increased our faith tremendously! Sometimes we have not because we ask not! *John 16:24 "Hitherto have ye asked nothing in my name: ask and ye shall receive, that your joy may be full."*

19

Enlarging Our Coasts

"... The harvest truly is plenteous, but the labourers are few........"
—Matthew 9:37

The move to Wyldewood Baptist Church in Oshkosh quickly proved that God's hand was upon it all the way. About six months after our move it became evident that we needed to rebuild the right engine on the Chieftain, which is a big job and requires some expertise. God knew this need was coming up and that we would need the help that was available out of Wyldewood. I can't praise God enough for the talented and qualified men that He gave us to accomplish this major task.

Craig Bloomer, who was a supervisor at Basler Turbo Conversions in Oshkosh and a member of Wyldewood Baptist Church, headed up the job. Other men from Wyldewood who worked with him on the engine removal and reinstalling and who were also employed at Basler included our son Gary, Dick Dempsey, and Fred Swanson. After William Randall's accident, Gary had taken his family to the island to help out there for a time, but he was now with us in Oshkosh. Randy Meyers, who was raised on a farm neighboring my brother Bill's in-laws' farm in Pequot Lakes, Minnesota, was now a manager at Basler. He had his inspector's license, was kind enough to sign off the work at no charge, saving the ministry many hundreds of dollars. Even our pastor got his hands dirty on the removal of the old engine. All these men, with the exception of Pastor King, were licensed aircraft mechanics. Other men also helped, and we were so grateful for the contribution of time and talent of each one.

One of the men whose help in the removal of the old engine was invaluable in a special way was Dan Johannes, from Heritage Baptist Church in Great Falls, Montana. Dan flew in to help us, and his father-in-law, Morris Thompson, who lives east of Madison, Wisconsin, came up with his truck and transported the engine to the overhaul shop near Rockford, Illinois. The contribution and giving spirit of both these men blesses my heart beyond words. I am so grateful!

I am also thankful to the management of Maxair, Inc., in Appleton, Wisconsin, the fixed base operation where we hangared the airplane for about five years, for allowing us the use of a corner of their maintenance shop and tools at no extra charge, as well as for their mechanics, who graciously assisted at times and put up with our occupying their work space. *Luke 6:38: "Give, and it shall be given unto you. .... "* I stand amazed at what God has done for us since we have been at Wyldewood Baptist Church. God certainly confirmed that our move was in his perfect will. His clear, plain path has been made obvious in so many ways! God is so good!

Shortly after our move to Oshkosh, Harry Winters and his family sold their home in Aurora, Colorado, and moved to the nearby small town of Omro in order to remain active in the Wings ministry. Since I had been a qualified DC-3 captain with Frontier Airlines, and Basler Flight Service was still flying DC-3s on cargo runs, I hired on with them as a part-time pilot to supplement our income, which at the time was a great help and blessing to us. I later also checked out in the Turbine DC-3 and flew it for a time as well. When Basler's Director of Flight Operations resigned, I was asked to fill that position while another man they had hired would work under my authority for three years to gain the qualifications necessary to assume the director position. Part of my pay would be hangar space for the Wings airplane. With that, we were able to move the Wings airplane to Oshkosh from Maxair in Appleton, which was a great blessing to all. Once again, we saw God's wonderful hand of provision for both the ministry and us personally.

My copilot and me with Turbine DC-3

Flying for Basler provided the opportunity for Gary and me to fly together, which was a lifelong memory-maker for the two of us. After Basler qualified Gary as a copilot on the DC-3, we had the privilege of flying several trips together, sometimes late at night. It was an unforgettable experience and a real joy flying with my own son.

Son Gary in right seat of DC-3

During my five years with Basler I experienced more engine shutdowns than in all my 27 years with Frontier Airlines. One of those experiences took place at 3:00 a.m. over Kentucky en route to Greenville, South Carolina. The copilot was flying, and I was half asleep when he yelled out that we had a fire in the right engine. I leaned forward and took a quick look. We immediately shut down the engine, and the fire went out. We called air traffic control and informed them of our problem, asking for a radar vector to the nearest suitable airport. The controller reminded us that we had just passed over the airport at Hazard, Kentucky, about 12 miles back. We were in the clear, though in an area where it was dark and there were very few lights on the ground. The Hazard airport is uncontrolled and unmanned at that time of night, and we had no way to get any detail about wind, runway conditions, or other information.

As we approached the airport, we clicked our mike on the Unicom frequency (a frequency for local airport information and runway lighting) and got the runway lights on, but no other information. On landing we had a right cross wind, and our right engine was shut down, making it difficult to keep the airplane traveling straight. As a result, we slowly crept toward the right side of the runway as we decelerated, and we came to a turn off taxiway just as our right main wheel reached the edge of the runway. We turned onto the taxiway and parked, since we could not taxi with one engine. We sat there until later in the morning when the airport manager showed up and hooked onto us with a tug and towed us to the ramp near the terminal. We contacted Basler, informing them of our problem, and then went to a hotel to rest and wait while parts and mechanics were flown in to fix the engine and we could fly the aircraft home. Such is the life of those who love flight!

* * * * * *

The year after our arrival in Oshkosh, Pastor King and I felt led by the Lord to start a conference during the week of the famous AirVenture airshow and fly-in, that we call the Meeting in the Air. This event opened a door of fellowship and encouragement to others through preaching and networking. We continue to hold the conference starting on the Wednesday evening of EAA week through Sunday night, with invited speakers each evening, most of whom are pilots. It has proven to be a great blessing to other Christian pilots and missionaries serving the Lord with aviation from all over the world, as well as to our own church family. Our new hangar would eventually be conveniently located on the airport grounds with a southern exposure, enabling visitors to the hangar to observe the daily EAA airshow from the comfort of the hangar.

****

A few years before our move to Oshkosh I had met Barton Case, pastor of Calvary Baptist Church in South Range, Michigan, at a missions conference in Park Rapids, where we presented the Wings ministry and gave plane rides to people at the conference. Bart booked a trip with Wings for himself and some of the men of his church, and over the next few years he would complete 11 trips with Wings. He eventually felt led to resign his church, move his family to Oshkosh, and join the Wings ministry in September of 2000.

Case family: Craig, Anna, William, Barton, Maria, Nancy

One memorable mission trip for Bart took place when Wings flew to Houghton, Michigan, to spend the night and leave the next morning with him, his wife, and a group of teens to work with missionary Greg Lambert and his family in Cadereyta, Nuevo Leon, Mexico. We arrived in Cadereyta on a Saturday afternoon, got acquainted with the missionary family, and settled into their home for the week. Sunday we participated in church services held in the missionary's garage and tried to adjust to the extreme heat and humidity.

Monday morning, we were awakened very early by a knock on the door. It was the local police telling us we had to evacuate the premises and go to another part of the city for safety. Apparently we were in danger of a major propane explosion. A propane storage area not far from the missionary's home was experiencing a fire, and there was the possibility of one or more of their large tanks exploding.

Of course we immediately left and drove to a safer area, where we found a local restaurant and decided to have some breakfast as long as we were out. We had a sweet time of fellowship and about five hours later we were allowed to return to the missionary's house, praising the Lord that there was no explosion and that no one was killed, although one of the workers at the propane plant was injured.

Propane tanks scorched by fire

Later Greg Lambert, Bart, and I went to survey the situation. When we arrived at the plant we saw the damage and could understand why the alarm was raised. A major shut off valve on one of the tanks had malfunctioned and caught fire. The three tanks at the site were scorched quite extensively, and it is amazing that none of them exploded.

That was a rather unusual way to start a busy week of activity. The teen group traveled to a nearby village where the Lamberts had established a small national church and where the teens cut down brush and did other work around the church building. Bart worked on the church van, which was in great disrepair. It had major problems with the brakes and brake lines, ignition switch, and carburetor, as well as flat tires. The roads there were rough and filled with potholes and had taken a serious toll on vehicles, and it was a challenge to even find vehicle parts, but he did what he could.

Wings also purchased materials and built kitchen cabinets and installed countertops for Mrs. Lambert, since her kitchen had neither. The teens passed out tracts in the community and had the opportunity to visit the local zoo. We discovered that one of the needs of the Lambert family at that time was the simple desire for fellowship, and the teens provided that for the Lambert youngsters, talking and laughing and playing games.

Also on this trip we learned when Bart and Greg Lambert went for a run on the nearby soccer field that the missionary owned only one pair of shoes, his dress shoes. He wore size 13W, which is nearly impossible to find in Mexico. Amazingly, Bart wore the same size and just "happened" to have purchased a brand new pair of tennis shoes for the trip. At the end of the week when we left the Lamberts to return home, Bart was thrilled to gift his almost new shoes to Pastor Lambert, thereby meeting a need only God could have known about and planned for.

Isaiah 65:24 . . . that before they call, I will answer; and while they are yet speaking, I will hear. That day this verse became a reality to us!

Two weeks later Bart was able to return to Cadereyta on another Wings trip with both the resources and vehicle parts provided by Calvary Baptist Church to again tackle the necessary repairs on that church van. After four days of work on the van, Bart and I were able to get the van into drivable condition, and the national pastor drove it off with a huge smile on his face and I'm sure praising God for his goodness.

Pastor Bart Case working on Mexican church van

* * * * * *

In 2002 Missionary Terry Rushing and his family attended our Meeting inthe Air Conference. He had been serving as a missionary in Uranium City, Saskatchewan, Canada, for 11 years, first with Mark Robertson, and a little later with Jim Pfaffenroth. Terry is an adopted, only child who felt a deep sense of responsibility toward his ailing parents, who lived in Arkansas and felt he must leave the ministry in Canada to care for them. He was also working part time as a mechanic for a local operation and as a pilot in Saskatchewan, flying the same type of aircraft that we have in the Wings ministry. Terry is a graduate of the Bob Jones University aviation program and is licensed as a pilot and mechanic in both the USA and Canada.

   I had been praying for some time that the Lord would bring a man to work with us with Terry's qualifications, and I asked him if he would consider doing some flying for Wings As Eagles until God gave him a clear direction for further ministry. He agreed, and God burdened his heart to join the Wings ministry in October of 2002. Terry was God's answer to my prayer.

Terry Rushing and family while serving in Uranium City

    I sent Terry, now the captain, on his first mission flight without me, going to Yellowknife, Northwest Territories, Canada. As I watched him board the aircraft with his mission team, start the engines, taxi to the runway, and take to the air, I was moved to tears with praise to our loving Lord, who had brought such a capable, qualified, godly, dedicated man to take over this ministry and lead it to higher heights. At the same time, I was moved with emotion over the fact that my days of flying these mission trips were now quickly coming to an end. Serving the Lord in this way had been my passion and my life since the beginning of the Wings ministry, but age had begun to take its toll, and I could see that God was preparing this younger man to eventually direct the ministry that God, by his grace, had allowed me to start.

    I praised God for modern technology that allowed me to observe his flight along the way to his mission field destination. This helped me to feel like I had a small part in the endeavor from home, and I could pray for them on their way.

    I still stand in awe at how our loving God has blessed and orchestrated this ministry and brought us godly, dedicated men and their families to carry the gospel to the regions beyond! Our move to Oshkosh certainly enabled us to enlarge our coasts.

* * * * * * *

For many years I had had a dream of starting a flight training program for aspiring missionary aviation pilots, and God laid on my heart the idea of a weeklong flight camp for young men ages fourteen to twenty to be conducted like a Bible camp, with an emphasis on aviation. I discussed the plan with Fred Swanson, who had helped us so willingly with the engine project. Fred, a qualified pilot, flight instructor, and aircraft mechanic, was excited about the idea and eager to have a part in making it happen. We began to make plans to hold the camp the week after the 2002 EAA fly-in; however, our blessed Lord had different plans for Fred.

In the spring of 2002 when Fred took a Basler Beech Bonanza for a test hop after an annual inspection, he ran into trouble and crashed on final approach to runway 36, immediately going to his eternal home with the Lord. We all have that appointment spoken of in Hebrews 9:27, and when God says come home, we go home! We are not promised another day! We are reminded that *"Precious in the sight of the Lord is the death of His saints" Psalm 116:15.* Fred left behind a wife and two young children. Ourhearts were broken over this loss, and we postponed our plans to start the flight camp that summer.

Later in the year 2002 I was in a missions conference in Appleton, Wisconsin, where a missionary by the name of Dave Spangler shared his ministry in the Bahama Islands. I quickly discovered that he was a pilot and flight instructor who owned and used a Cessna-172 in his ministry for traveling from the Florida mainland to the Bahama Islands to hold preaching services and vacation Bible schools. At my first opportunity I talked with him, sharing my vision for a flight camp for high school boys and asked if he would consider coming up to Oshkosh with his airplane to help us. He was very excited about the novel idea and agreed to help launch the Wings As Eagles first flight camp in the summer of 2003, flying into Oshkosh with his Cessna-172 to provide flight instruction and missionary preaching.

Cessna-172 used for flight camp

Gene Zastera, another member of Wyldewood and an A&P and avionics instructor at Fox Valley Technical College in Oshkosh, arranged to use Fox Valley's facilities at no charge during camp week to offer some basic training to flight campers. Things were coming together, and the last week of July 2003 Wings As Eagles Flight Camp took off with nine campers. It was a great success, with God's blessing, and Flight Camp has grown bigger and better each year. Several of our campers have since gone into fulltime missionary aviation ministries as pilots and aircraft mechanics.

Gene Zastera teaching campers

Flight Camp engine test station, Terry Rushing, and campers

After about three years of bringing his airplane to Flight Camp, missionary Dave Spangler bought a Piper Aztec for his ministry and sold us the Cessna-172, which we have since upgraded with a new paint job, new interior, and many other upgrades, mostly all donated. We still use that aircraft for our camp and other training today. *God is so good!*

The following is an excerpt from a letter that one of our early flight campers sent to Wings following his week at camp:

> Not only was this flight camp fun and exciting, but it also was one of the most spiritually uplifting times in my entire life. During my senior year I had started to make the wrong friends, and, as you can probably guess, things just went downhill from there as I got involved in the wrong things, and cars and racing became my idols.
>
> The only reason that I attended Flight Camp is that I was pretty interested in aviation, and my grandpa convinced me to come. He said that it would be really good for me, and now I know what he meant. The day that I left for camp, I had all the wrong

friends, bad influences in my life, and a heart (very regrettably) that was not right with God Almighty.

I think that there was no other place that God would rather have me be that week than Flight Camp. I learned so much about aviation, mechanics, the Wings As Eagles ministry, and so many spiritual truths as well. One of the things that really got me was when Brother Tobin spoke about how we all are prisoners of either Christ, ourselves, or the devil. At that moment I realized that God had me here for a purpose, and that I needed to do a serious 180 degree turn around before it was too late.

Flight Camp week was a total revival for me in my personal walk with God. It was really something that I had <u>no</u> idea would happen. It was a real blessing to have all of the great fellowship, and to be fed from the Word of God. In short, this week was nothing but a blessing, and if I hadn't come, I know that I would only have drifted farther from God.

Flight Camp class of 2014

As we continued full speed ahead in the Wings ministry, the need for our own hangar facilities was becoming more and more apparent. We started actively praying and fundraising for this project in 2001. By April of 2004 we had leased land at the end of the taxiway Hotel and were working on the permit process. God's people continued to support and give to the project, and we broke ground for an 80x80-foot hangar in May 2004. We call it the Eagle's Nest. It has room for the Chieftain and several other aircraft. The hangar also is equipped with a restroom, a shower room, refrigerator, coffee table area, computer, and flight simulator. It is a pleasant place to relax and work. We were able to move into our own hangar almost the very day that my contract with Basler ended. God wonderfully supplied the Eagle's Nest with the necessary tools and supplies, including the acoustical interior side walls and many other materials graciously donated. *Only God!*

Hangar ground breaking

Completed foundation

The Eagle's Nest

During the years we were getting settled in our new environment in Oshkosh and expanding the scope of the ministry, the mission trips to foreign countries continued, with Wings groups serving missionaries in Mexico, Canada, Grand Turk Island, Dominican Republic, and Honduras.

* * * * * *

On September 10, 2001, we had just started a mission trip. We had spent the night at the Bearing Precious Seed base in El Paso, Texas, and were planning to leave for Guerrero, Chihuahua, Mexico, the following morning. Arising early on September 11 and preparing to leave for the airport, we were told to go back in and check the TV news, which we did. We listened in shock and disbelief to the reports about the attack on the twin towers in New York City. Our flight into Mexico was canceled, and we were grounded in El Paso for a number of days before we were allowed to take to the air again to fly home to Oshkosh. While we were grounded at the BPS base in Texas, God used us to help assemble scriptures and assist with vehicle and building maintenance.

20

The Mighty Hand of God

"For whether we live, we live unto the Lord; and whether we die, we die unto the Lord........."—Romans 14:8

When we traveled to Mexico through Laredo, Texas, we usually arrived in Laredo too late to continue into Mexico the same day, so in the early years of the Wings ministry we became acquainted with Missionary Bill Waldrop and his ministry Rio Grande Missionary Help in Laredo. Many times we landed in Laredo, where Brother Waldrop would pick us up at the airport and take us to a restaurant for our evening meal, and then to the church that he pastored, where we would spend the night. Bill Waldrop was always so helpful and accommodating, and we appreciated our relationship with him and his family so much. His son-in-law Kelle Hein was also a missionary on the US/Mexico border and Bill Waldrop's righthand man.

Bill and Carolyn Waldrop

Over time Bill needed to expand his work of providing housing and assistance to missionaries coming in and out of Mexico for mail and supplies, as the facilities at the church were becoming inadequate. The Lord led him to a property on the east side of Laredo, and he entered into a building project, which eventually included a home, dormitories, dining hall, eleven motel-type units which he called Shepherds Inn, and other facilities. Wings As Eagles had the privilege of taking many work crews to help with this project beginning in the year 2000.

Shepherds Inn under construction

Mrs. Karen Stertz, one of our Wyldewood church ladies, has been a huge blessing to the Wings ministry ever since our arrival in Oshkosh. She wanted to get involved with the ministry, and started a ministry she called Wings Outreach Ministry. At that time, she was a manager at a Subway restaurant, and she got permission to supply each Wings As Eagles mission flight with Subway sandwiches free of charge. She also collected many donations from other local businesses for the missionaries with whom we were going to serve. As part of the Outreach Ministry, she gathered together a number of ladies to quilt blankets for the Rio Grande Missionary Help motel units and create other items to decorate the rooms.

When the projects of building and decorating were complete, Bill Waldrop wrote the following note of appreciation:

It would be impossible to express our feelings of love and appreciation to you for all you have done for this ministry. Likewise, we know that it is impossible for us to reward you, but it is a blessing to know our great God, who knows all and rewards all and is aware of everything that has been accomplished. For now, please accept our love and gratitude to you for your love and labor for him.

I can only praise the Lord when I walk around the grounds and observe what is there. What a blessing! Wings has touched so many lives and has so much physical testimony in so many different mission fields so that the gospel message will continue to be given out until he comes again. A special thanks to your wife and other loved ones who suffered the loss of your presence while you were here.

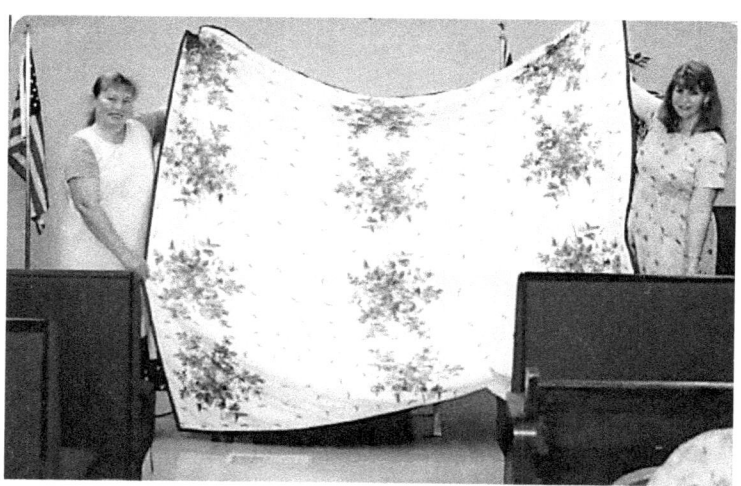

Karen Stertz, left, and Mrs. Kelle Hein holding blanket for motel unit

Kelle Hein pastored Family Baptist Church in Laredo and was also a pilot and flight instructor. In March of 2018 Kelle was in the right pilot seat in a Piper Navajo with a young man in the left seat doing the flying. They had just taken off from Laredo, headed for San Antonio, when they had engine trouble and, in their attempt to return to the Laredo airport, they crashed on the airport proper. The aircraft burst into flames, and both men were killed instantly. Kelle, of course, went home to be with the Lord, but we have no knowledge of the young man's spiritual condition. Kelle's homegoing was a great loss to his family, his church, his father-in-law Bill Waldrop, and Rio Grande Missionary Help, as well as to all of us who knew and loved him. Sometimes it is hard not to ask why, but we must instead trust.

Bart Case was driving on his way to the Waldrops' to help him for a week, and he was just an hour and a half north of Laredo at the time of the accident. God used him in a wonderful way to comfort and encourage the family. Kelle's children were all grown and on their own at that time, but the sudden loss of a parent at any age has an impact on a family. His dear wife Tammy was left to adjust to being alone. Tammy continues to serve faithfully with her parents at Rio Grande Missionary Help.

21

A Table in the Wilderness

"So he fed them according to the integrity of his heart; and guided them by the skilfulness of his hands."—Psalm 78:72

In March of 2002 we had the privilege of flying a trip to Farmington, New Mexico, to take part in the historical dedication of the just completed Navajo Nation New Testament translation of the Bible, printed by Bearing Precious Seed printing work in Milford, Ohio. At that time twin brothers Ron and Don Corley and their wives had ministered to the Navajo Indians for about 40 years and had been involved in the translation. On board the Wings aircraft were Pastor Freddy McMillen and wife Jody, Bearing Precious Seed missionaries Jim and Monica Hoffman and son Ben, and my wife Juanita. What an exciting time of celebration it was, and what a blessing to see for the first time in history the Navajo Nation possess the New Testament in their language. President Begay of the Navajo Nation, who is a saved man, was there and gave an eloquent acceptance speech. What a God we serve!

* * * * * * *

A remarkable incident that allowed God to show His grace in a mighty way happened on November 4, 2002, when we were on our way to Laredo, Texas, for an overnight at Rio Grande Missionary Help facility before going on to Durango, Mexico, to work with national pastor Arturo Garza for a week. We had made a fuel stop at Mineral Wells, Texas, and taken off with full fuel and all seats filled. We had been in flight about thirty minutes, cruising at six thousand feet headed for Laredo, when things began to happen.

The RPM on the left engine began to oscillate severely. Our engine monitor showed that the number five cylinder was dead. I was able to stabilize the RPM while keeping an eye on pressures and temperatures. My first thought was to continue to Laredo, which was about an hour's flight, but then I noticed the oil pressure dropping and the oil temperature rising. I feathered the left engine propeller, advised air traffic control of our problem, and told them that I wanted to proceed directly to San Antonio. We were cleared to San Antonio and told to descend to 4000 feet. We were having a little trouble maintaining altitude, so I punched the nearest airport button on the GPS and saw that an airport with a 6000-foot paved runway was eight miles straight ahead. I thought at the time that it was the Johnson City Municipal Airport, and we were headed straight for it.

We were in the clouds with light rain, and the airport had no approach facilities. Knowing that every airport has a certain clearway around it, I decided to cross over the airport and spiral down. Bart Case was sitting in the right seat as my copilot, and I asked him to keep an eye open and let me know when he saw something. I completed one turn to the right, and he spotted the runway through a hole in the clouds. I made one more turn and broke out of the clouds at about 300 feet. Seeing the runway, I lined up and landed safely. Keeping our speed up, I was able to taxi to the far end of the runway and pull off near a hangar.

I parked and discovered that I was unable to contact San Antonio approach control. I heard a Southwest Airline flight talking to the San Antonio approach, and I asked him to report that we were safely on the ground in Johnson City. I turned around and asked our preacher on board, Pastor Buhrow, to thank God that we were safely on the ground. We all deplaned, a green van drove up and a man in a park ranger uniform got out.

"Who's the pilot?" he asked. I told him that I was the pilot. "Do you have any idea where you are?" he asked.

"Yes, sir," I replied. "We are in Johnson City, Texas!"

"It used to be the Johnson City Municipal Airport, but it is and has been for several years the private LBJ Ranch!" he said.

Lyndon B. Johnson hadn't crossed my mind for years, so it took me a few seconds to comprehend who he was talking about, but when I understood, in my mind I could see the Secret Service, the FBI, the FAA, and only God knows who else I might have to answer to for landing where we had—though technically in an emergency a pilot can do whatever is necessary for safety.

The man in uniform asked us to get into his van, and he transported us to the park headquarters. The LBJ property where LBJ was raised had become both a state and national historic park, but the runway was his private property, not open to the public. We were of course then asked to identify ourselves and explain where we were going and what our plan was. Everyone who dealt with us was very kind and cordial, and after the questioning was complete about 4 p.m., they asked us what we wanted to do. We replied that we needed to find a place to stay for the night and were told that there was a motel in Johnson City, the Saved Inn. The ranger who had picked us up offered to take us there.

"I normally never drive this van, but for some reason this morning I decided to drive it," he said as we got in. *God knew!* I thought.

"I would be glad to take you to the motel," he continued. "But first, let me give you a little tour of the ranch." Our ranger drove us around the property and showed us the home where LBJ and his wife Lady Bird spent their time when not in Washington. They pastured Black Angus cattle and had several other small homes where they housed employees.

Upon checking into the Saved Inn, I contacted our friend Bill Waldrop in Laredo, informed him of our plight, and asked him if he would consider driving to Johnson City to pick us up and allow our group to use his van to continue our mission trip to Durango.

"Whatever it takes!" he replied cheerfully. "I'll be there in about four hours." His plan was to pick up our group and return to Laredo that night, but instead we got him a room and convinced him to stay in Johnson City and leave after breakfast the next morning.

Bart Case and I decided to stay back in Johnson City and try to determine the problem with the airplane and see it taken care of. After breakfast our group left with Bill Waldrop while Bart and I tried to find a rental car that we could use to return to the LBJ Ranch. We soon discovered that there were no rental car services in Johnson City. We walked a couple blocks up the street to a convenience store and gas station where a little Mexican lady behind the counter asked us how she could help. I told her about our problem and asked if she knew of any place where we could rent or borrow a vehicle.

"Here," she said, and reached over the counter and handed me a set of keys. "You can borrow my truck. It's sitting out front." She nodded toward a relatively new Ford pickup parked outside. "All I ask is that you're back by 3:00 so I can pick up my kid from school."

Bart and I nearly fainted, but we could see the hand of God working out the details, and there was much more to come.

We took her keys, and while getting into the truck we noticed that her purse was on the seat, so I took it inside to her saying, "I'm sure you want this."

"Oh yes!" she said. "Thank you so very much! And by the way, don't bother putting gas in it, because I get gas free here."

I told her thank you, gave her our names, and promised to have the truck back by 3:00.

Back at LBJ Ranch, we were greeted by the head park ranger. "I understand you had a little problem here last night," he said. "What would you like to do?"

We explained our situation and told him that we wanted to find an aircraft mechanic who could help us determine the problem and know if we would be looking at an engine change.

"I don't have anything else demanding of my time right now," he said. "I'd be glad to take you to Fredericksburg, about fifteen miles to the west, where I know we could find a mechanic."

Sure enough, at the airport in Fredericksburg we found a mechanic who was willing to go back and look at the airplane for us. Upon examination, we discovered that we had dropped a valve in the number five cylinder, and it would definitely require an engine change. The park ranger advised us to contact LBJ's grandson, who was in charge of the airstrip.

When I contacted Mr. Nugent, he said, "I heard you had a little problem there last night. What can I do for you?"

"If possible, I'd like to move the airplane across the runway and tie it down on the west side," I said.

"Would you like to hangar it?" he asked.

"You have a hangar that we could put it in?" I replied in surprise.

"The hangar you're parked in front of just has a few four wheelers and a hunting truck in it. If you contact my partner Barney Hulett, he'll move those things out, and you are more than welcome to put the airplane inside for as long as you need it."

We contacted Barney, and he said he would meet us at the hangar at 8:00 the next morning, at which time we moved the airplane inside. After we thanked Barney, we arranged to rent a car and drive to Laredo to wait for our group to return from Durango.

In the meantime, we contacted Pastor King and arranged for a couple of men to drive the church van to Laredo to return our group to Oshkosh. Those men drove straight through to Laredo, about seventeen hours, and after a day's rest they transported our entire group back to Oshkosh.

After our return home we contacted Firewall Forward, an engine overhaul shop in Fort Collins, Colorado, and discovered that the manager Mark Seader was a brother in Christ who belonged to an independent Baptist church. He offered us a $10,000 discount on the overhaul job, and we arranged to get the work done in Fort Collins. Now of course we needed a pickup truck to drive back to Texas, remove the engine, and then transport it to Fort Collins.

While I was at LBJ Ranch, Juanita had been to our dentist, Dr. Tom Dowling, who is also a Christian, and when he asked about me, she told him about our situation. He offered us his pickup if we needed one. After exhausting other possibilities, I contacted Dr. Dowling, and he was more than willing to loan us his almost new pickup to make the 4000-mile trip.

Terry Rushing had just recently joined the Wings As Eagles ministry at that time and was with his parents in Arkansas. I drove the pickup from Oshkosh to Arkansas, where I picked up Terry, and we continued to the LBJ Ranch, once again staying at the Saved Inn. Working with Mr. Hulett, we arranged to get into the hangar to remove the engine. With the help of one of the park rangers and a forklift, we had the engine loaded into the pickup by late afternoon, at which time we started our trip to the overhaul shop in Fort Collins. We dropped off the engine, and

I drove Terry to Omaha, Nebraska, where he caught a bus back to Arkansas, and I drove back to Oshkosh.

Terry Rushing preparing engine for removal

Terry and fork lift operator loading engine

Terry and Barney securing engine

The overhaul took about five weeks to complete. In late December the shop called and told us that the engine was about finished and that we could arrange to pick it up. John Douglas, who worked for Basler and had become director of maintenance for Wings, along with his family and me, took the church van and headed for Fort Collins. I was driving while John and his family slept. It was about 3:00 a.m. and I was fighting sleep, with about ten miles to go to Grand Island, Nebraska, where I planned to let John take over the driving, when I blinked one too many times and fell asleep, the van leaving the freeway and going into the median. I abruptly woke up and after a few gyrations managed to steer the van back onto the freeway and get things under control with nothing hurt.

John woke up and yelled, "What's going on?!"

I pulled over to the side of the road and let him take over. God once again was merciful and spared us!

When we arrived in Cheyenne, Wyoming, our daughter Lisa, who lived north of Denver, picked me up, while John and family continued to Rock Springs, Wyoming, to visit his wife's family. I planned to call him when the engine was ready, and he would meet me at the overhaul shop in Fort Collins with the van.

John Douglas and family

Several days later, when John and I met at Firewall Forward to pick up the engine, the work was still a couple hours from being finished, and while we were waiting, I walked around the van and saw a nail sticking out of the right rear tire. We took the van to a shop in Fort Collins, and in the process of fixing the tire, the mechanics found that the axle seal on that same side was also leaking. By God's grace, they had the parts and fixed the leaking seal as well. Had the Lord not directed my eyes to see that nail, John and I may well have broken down somewhere along the way on our all-night trip to LBJ Ranch.

We had to be at the ranch before noon the next day so that someone would be available to operate the forklift needed to hang the engine back on the aircraft. We arrived just in time!! We worked that afternoon and all the next day getting everything hooked up and running. After a short test hop, I departed with the airplane for Oshkosh, and John drove the van back to Rock Springs to pick up his family and drive home to Oshkosh.

Mr. Hulett had been a military pilot and had flown for Presidents Dwight Eisenhower through Lyndon Johnson. He flew Lyndon Johnson to the hospital when he died of a heart attack. We invited him to our Wings banquet, held the Saturday of our Meeting in the Air conference the following year, and honored him for the part that he had in getting the Wings As Eagles ministry back in the air.

Barney Hulett and his wife

This experience was such a faith builder for me, as I saw the mighty hand of God work out every detail. The Lord gave us many opportunities to share the gospel and to encourage others with this story. I believe the devil attempted to destroy this ministry, but God turned it around for good, and the kingdom of heaven was advanced with many lives being touched with the gospel as a result of our near accident. To God be the glory! Had we made it to San Antonio when the engine failed instead of to the LBJ Ranch, it undoubtedly would have cost us a small fortune before we were finished. After almost two months in their hangar and all the help so willingly given at the ranch, they were very gracious to not charge us! Can God set a table in the wilderness? Through this adventure He proved that he certainly can.

22

To the Work

". . . So they strengthened their hands for this good work."
—Nehemiah 2:18

Doug Kalapp, our director of church relations at the time, became very involved in the missions program at First Baptist Church, and also taught missions classes at the College. As a result, his heart was drawn to the countries of China, the Philippines, and India. Doug confessed to me that it was one of the hardest decisions he ever had to make, but finding it impossible to do justice to both ministries, he tendered his resignation from Wings As Eagles in the fall of 2002 to devote his time to the missions program at his church. He had been used by God in the Wings work and contributed a great deal to the ministry, and we missed him greatly!

Doug had experienced some health issues related to his heart, and a few years later the Lord called him home, leaving his dear wife Karen alone. By this time their children were grown, married, and on their own.

About eight years later, Mrs. Kalapp sent me a check to pay for the motor home I had given them to travel in twenty-eight years before. I called and told her that I hadn't thought about them owing us for the motorhome in many years and that her check was not necessary. She told me that God had blessed her and that she wanted us to have the money; we might have need for it someday. I, of course, thanked her as best I knew how, and asked God to continue to bless her abundantly.

About a month later during our Meeting in the Air conference, one of our visiting preachers borrowed our car and had an accident at a four-way stop near our church. Juanita and I had been to a grocery store and were headed for the church a few cars behind our preacher friend. Traffic was stopped, and I suggested to Juanita that there must have been an accident ahead. As the traffic began to move and we reached the four-way stop, we saw that there was indeed an accident and that one of the cars involved was ours. I couldn't believe it! We pulled over, and I went back to check on the preacher. He was hurting a little, so we took him to the emergency area at the hospital nearby. He was bruised, but not seriously hurt, so we took him to church for the evening service.

Our car was totaled, and little did we or Mrs. Kalapp know at the time that the money she had sent to us would be needed along with the insurance settlement to purchase a replacement vehicle. Once again, God provided before we even knew to ask! *"And it shall come to pass, that before they call, I will answer; and while they are yet speaking, I will hear."* Isaiah 65:24, what an amazing God we serve!

A few weeks later Mrs. Kalapp called and asked for our prayers, informing us that a widowed, retired preacher had called her and wanted to get acquainted. That relationship developed, and Karen is now very happily married once again. God knows our needs, and he deeply cares!!

* * * * * *

Early in the spring of 2005 Jim Pfaffenroth brought us a four-place PiperPacer that had to be stripped to the frame and completely rebuilt to be used in his ministry in Uranium City, Saskatchewan, Canada. God had wonderfully supplied the personnel and knowhow to do the aircraft rebuild, and we now had the facility in which to accomplish the project. John Douglas, who had become our director of maintenance by that time, headed up the project, with all of us getting involved when we could. God thus expanded our ministry into aircraft rebuilding and maintenance for other servants of the Lord using aviation to reach the lost. The Pacer was finished and better than new by July 2006, and Terry flew it on its first flight after the rebuild. What a beautiful sight it was to behold as he lifted off and climbed out! Everything ran well, and very few finetuning adjustments were required, indicating a job well done. The next day Terry left on the long flight delivering the aircraft to Uranium City, arriving there without any problems. Praise the sweet Lord!

I appreciate so very much the long hours, dedication, and sacrifice by all who had a part in this project! John Douglas, Terry Rushing, and Dave Borlee, a mechanic for Basler and a fellow member of Wyldewood, gave all they could to see this huge project through to completion with the help of others who did what they could as time allowed. Dave has been a faithful friend and servant to the Wings ministry now for many years. I appreciate so much the sacrifice of the families who, with patience and without complaint, allowed their husbands and fathers to serve as unto the Lord. God has certainly brought to us some wonderful and talented families with whom to serve.

Pacer ready for delivery

At the Meeting in the Air the last week of July 2006, Missionary Tom Needham on furlough from Cameroon, Africa, told me that a church in Oregon had given him a Sportsman home build project, and he was wondering where he could build the aircraft for his ministry in Cameroon. We had just finished the Pacer, and space in the hangar was available again, so I suggested that he bring the project to Oshkosh, and we would help him with it. He was overwhelmingly grateful for that invitation, and in September, when the project was delivered to the Wings hangar, work began immediately. Tom had six months to personally work on the project before he had to return to Cameroon.

Tom Needham and son Daniel looking over the Sportsman project

The work on the Sportsman was accomplished by May 2007, and plans to fly the plane to Cameroon were set in place. John Douglas volunteered to make the incredible flight across the Atlantic, which required extensive planning, and, on John's part, some real courage, faith, and endurance for the long, lonely flight across many miles of open water. Tom Needham had to reapply for permission to fly his aircraft in Cameroon, and as of October that permission had not yet been granted. Therefore, the airplane was still in our hangar as the season for flying across the Atlantic closed, and the delivery to Cameroon was delayed until at least the next spring.

Tom Needhams' permission to fly in Cameroon did not come through until July 2008, so he and John began to make plans to fly across the Atlantic in September. Extra fuel tanks were installed in the right seat and rear seat of the cabin, giving a total range of about 15 hours of flight time instead of the usual five to six hours. John took off from Oshkosh and flew to Canada, then from Canada to the Azores, on to Northern Africa, and finally south to Cameroon. His total flying time was 42 flight hours, with the longest leg 12 hours from Canada to the Azores. The flight was completed safely, with no problems with the airplane or weather. What an amazing trip and experience! Another project completed to the glory of God!

THE OTHER WING

Sportsman fitted with long-range fuel tanks for delivery to Cameroon

In late October, 2008, Terry and his wife Sarah, along with several others, traveled to Cameroon by commercial flight to minister with the Needham's until November 11. Sharing the gospel and seeing people trust Christ as their Savior during that time was their greatest joy. Terry had the opportunity to do some African jungle flying while there, which was a new experience for him.

* * * * * * *

In early 2009 Terry Rushing, Bart Case, and I were on a mission trip with several others to Calvillo, Mexico. Terry flew captain and I flew co-pilot on the way down. We carry two sets of keys to the airplane, one set for the captain and the other set for whoever is copilot. We landed in Aquascalientes, where missionary Marvin Tobin picked us up and drove us to Calvillo, about 50 miles to the west. When we arrived at the church in Calvillo where we would be staying for the week, I handed Bart my set of keys, because the plan was for him to fly in the right seat on our return trip.

Church building in Calvillo

We had a great week, accomplished much work on a building project, and had good fellowship with the believers there. Marvin and Sandy Tobin were always a great blessing to be with and to minister with. They loved their people and that love was demonstrated unmistakably through their lives.

Missionaries Marvin and Sandy Tobin

At week's end, as we packed up for our return to Aquascalientes and our flight home, Captain Rushing asked, "Who has the other set of keys?"

"I gave them to Bart," I replied.

"I don't have them," Bart said.

"Yes, you do, Bart," I said. "I remember giving them to you when we got here."

"No, you didn't, and I don't have them!"

"Bart, you *do* have them," I said again. "I distinctly remember giving them to you on our arrival here at the church!"

"I'm telling you," Bart insisted. "I don't have them!"

I knew I had given him the keys and, in any case, I was certain they were no longer in my possession! We went back and forth about the keys in the van all the way back to Aquascalientes, and the last remark I had for Bart was, "Well, you are going to feel pretty stupid when you get home and find those keys in your possession!"

Back home in Oshkosh, in the process of unpacking my bag, I nearly fainted when I found the keys. Right there, in my bag. I had so clearly remembered handing them to Bart! So, I had to eat humble pie and call Bart to apologize and admit that I had found the keys in my bag. That was probably the hardest phone call that I have ever had to make! It has since become a standing joke and a story that gets told and laughed about to this day. When there is a question asked about something, it so often comes out, *Who has the keys?*

23

Trust in Him

"Behold, I give unto you power . . . and nothing shall by any means hurt you."— Luke 10:19

In November of 2010 missionary Earl Malpass invited me to fly with him from Oshkosh, Wisconsin, to Fairbanks, Alaska. Earl had just had both engines and propellers overhauled on his newly purchased Piper Navajo Chieftain and was ready to fly it to Fairbanks. Since I had extensive experience in the Chieftain, for safety's sake he wanted me to accompany him on that first long flight. We invited Bart Case to go along since he was free at that time, and Bart is always a handy man to have along.

We departed Oshkosh and landed in Regina, Saskatchewan, Canada, our first stop, to clear customs and refuel. Then we departed for Grand Prairie, Alberta, where we would spend the night. The next morning when we got our weather briefing before departure, our briefer informed us that a snow storm was building along our route, but that we should be able to fly over it and outrun it before we arrived at Whitehorse, Yukon Territories, our next stop. We topped off the fuel tanks, giving us five hours and 45 minutes total flight time. It would be the longest leg of the journey. Earl filed a flight plan to Whitehorse, and we departed. We climbed to our cruising altitude of 12,000 feet with an outside temperature of -25 degrees Fahrenheit.

We had been in snow showers now and then but were able to have ground contact most of the time. About 45 minutes out of Whitehorse we noticed that the oil pressure on the left engine was dropping, the oil temperature was rising above normal, and the outside air temperature was very cold. Earl had been advised that the heavier break-in oil would be all right for the flight to Fairbanks; however, there was no doubt that we were experiencing oil congealing because of low air temperatures. I yelled over the engine noise to Bart and told him to pray, for we had an engine problem. He looked and yelled back that he could see oil streaks on the engine cowling.

A few miles back Earl had noticed that we passed a landing strip in Teslin, and though he was reluctant to turn back, in order to save the engine, we feathered the propeller, shut down the left engine, and made a 180-degree turn to return to the strip we had just flown over. Teslin would be a beautiful village to stop in while driving through on a summer road trip, but it was not great for landing in November during a snowstorm, though at this time it was just light snow with fairly good visibility. No one was answering on the Unicom frequency, so Earl called the air traffic control center and asked them to call the airport attendant on the land line and get him to turn on some lights. He thought of requesting a fresh pot of coffee too, but thought better of it.

The terrain was mountainous, and we were high as we arrived over the snow-covered airstrip, so we made a right turn, keeping the airport facility in sight and continuing to descend as we watched for the runway lights for landing. Praise the Lord, as Earl was leveling the wings from the turn, we could see the lights showing from our angle. Snow had blocked them from being seen from overhead. All three of us yelled at the same time, "There they are!"

"Hang on, we have only one shot at this!" Earl said loudly enough for Bart to hear behind us. Lining up with the runway, we made a safe landing at Teslin, Yukon Territories, and praised the Lord for his wonderful mercy and grace.

After landing, Earl turned the aircraft around, but it was impossible to taxi on one engine, so we contacted the airport attendant on Unicom and asked if he could come out with a truck and strap to tow us up to the administration building ramp, which he did. After deplaning we entered the administration building, taking the extra cans of oil we had on board and placing them on the furnace to heat them up.

Almost immediately a young man came in from outside and said, "I'm looking for Earl Malpass." A friend of Earl's had been monitoring our journey online and saw us turn back. Believing we were having trouble and were returning to the airstrip we had just passed, he called the pastor of a church in Teslin that he happened to know and sent him to check on us in case we needed help. After we had a short conversation with the pastor and exchanged phone numbers with him, the pastor left. We put the now heated oil in the engines and started them. Everything was running fine, so we departed for Whitehorse, where we could get further help. Upon arrival in Whitehorse about 45 minutes later, we parked at an FBO (Fixed Base Operation), and a mechanic there offered to let Earl use his tools if needed.

Teslin Administration Building in Yukon Territories

Earl contacted Pastor Harrison of Calvary Baptist Church, who so graciously and helpfully loaned us a van to get around and allowed us to stay at the church for the next couple of days while we did the necessary maintenance to complete our trip to Fairbanks. What a great blessing it is to find God's people on life's journey who are willing to give of themselves and their resources to assist fellow servants along the way.

After a night's rest we went back to the airport. Unable to find an available hangar in which to work, and with the outside temperature well below zero, we managed to rent a portable space heater and insulated tarps to create tents over the engines. This was by no means ideal, but it gave us a warm place to work and heat the engines and enabled us to drain the oil and replace it with a lower viscosity oil that would eliminate the chance of its congealing during flight. Bart was a huge help to Earl in performing this maintenance function. God knew we needed him along!

After we completed our work on the plane, we enjoyed a time of fellowship with the pastor and a good night's rest. The next morning, we were airborne once again to complete our trip to Fairbanks. It was a beautiful day, the terrain all the way to Fairbanks was spectacular, and we were relieved that the remainder of our flight and arrival in Fairbanks were uneventful.

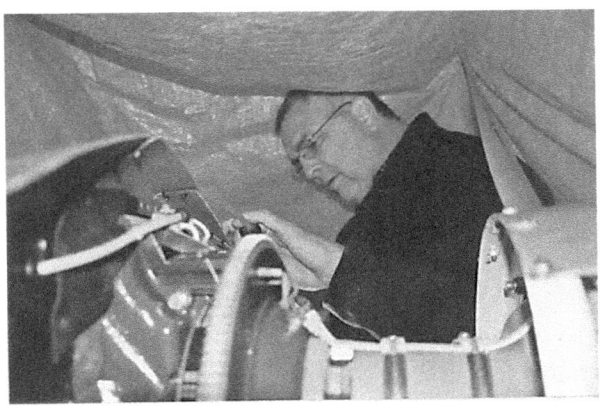

Bart Case performing maintenance

Bart and I spent a couple of days with Earl and his dear family before heading home to Oshkosh. Earl showed us around the town of North Pole, Alaska, a town of about 2000 people 14 miles southeast of Fairbanks. We saw intricate ice sculpture displays in the town—beautiful works of art! After a great meal prepared by Earl's wife, followed by an evening of fellowship and a good night's rest, Earl took us to the Fairbanks airport terminal, where Bart and I caught our commercial flight to make our way back to Oshkosh. We serve a great and mighty, loving, caring God!

Ice sculptures in North Pole, Alaska

24

A New Role

*"Ye have seen . . . how I bare you on eagles' wings,
and brought you unto myself."*—Exodus 19:4

At our 2009 Wings As Eagles board meeting, I announced that Juanita and I needed to back away from the directorship of the ministry. We had been wonderfully blessed with the privilege of being led of the Lord to start the Wings As Eagles ministry and direct its activities for many years, but now, due to our age and health issues, it was becoming clear that it was time to allow our "Timothy" to step up and take control under God's guidance. I planned to resign as Wings Director effective July 2010, and we needed to choose a new director for the ministry. A short discussion ensued, and the board cast a vote, with Terry Rushing being elected the next director to lead the Wings ministry to yet higher heights. The official transfer of directorship duties would take place in July 2010.

We planned a silver anniversary celebration banquet for Wings As Eagles for the last day of our annual Meeting in the Air in 2010, with family and ministry friends invited from many states and foreign countries. We were served a delicious meal, consisting of roast chicken breast with all the trimmings, served by our Wyldewood teens. The guests enjoyed a film, which featured interviews with Bob and Juanita Warinner and highlighted the 25 years of Wings As Eagles ministry. Missionary Jim Pfaffenroth blessed us with a challenging message from the Word of God, and we had a special ceremony transferring leadership of the ministry to now Captain Terry Rushing. It was a wonderfully blessed time, and Juanita and I were completely surprised when Pastor King presented us with a silver 2007 Toyota Camry to replace our blue 1989 Camry, and we could not hold back the tears as we were given the keys. We had no idea that such an incredible blessing had been prepared by family and friends of the ministry for the occasion.

Juanita and me receiving gift of the Camry

As we look back to where we started, Juanita and I continue to be humbled and overwhelmed with emotion to see how God is continuing to use the Wings ministry today. God launched us into the ministry years ago with a vision, a small airplane, a first church taking us on for 15 dollars per month, and just the two of us seeking to follow the Lord, not even able to devote ourselves to the ministry full time. Over the past 25 years, God has guided us step by step, encouraging and enabling us to follow wherever he led us, strengthening our faith and providing for our every need. He has allowed us to upgrade from a small, four-place airplane to our present ten-place aircraft and another four-place aircraft that we use for the flight camp and other ministry needs. We built our own hangar and along the way have flown 176 mission trips to Mexico, Honduras, the West Indies, Dominican Republic, Haiti, the Bahamas, and Canada. Wings personnel have also taken airline mission trips to Cameroon, Papua New Guinea, Australia, China, India, and the Philippines. Wings As Eagles' first missionary pilot, Sam Sanderlin, is on the field of Cameroon, Africa.

Wings has been involved in runway construction, transporting and delivering Scriptures, supplying medical and construction teams, flying medevac and relief flights, rebuilding and repairing missionary aircraft, preaching, evangelism, vacation Bible schools, and encouraging and supporting missionaries. God gave us the opportunity to touch many lives through these trips, and their lives have touched ours. Only God knows the whole story and the results of all that the Wings ministry has accomplished for his glory throughout these past twenty-five years. I am very grateful that God has allowed me and my family to have a part in sharing the gospel around the world. We are keenly aware of the fact that none of it could ever have been a reality without the help of God's people. They have responded to the leading of the Holy Spirit to support this ministry with their prayers and generous giving.

God has wonderfully blessed, but the time has come for new and younger leadership. I have continued as a board member and am ready to help in any capacity needed. Terry still calls me for advice from time to time. Juanita and I counsel young, struggling married couples, give out tracts, and share the gospel, as God gives opportunity. In some ways, I am back where I started summers ago in Nisswa, Minnesota—mowing the grass and trimming the shrubs in the summertime. Our roles have changed, but our desire is to be faithful to the Lord wherever He leads us in the days ahead.

Epilogue

As we prepare this manuscript for publication and I reflect on my 67-year flying career, I could never have imagined how God would work when I answered his call to be the other wing and launched the Wings As Eagles ministry. WAE is now in its thirty-sixth year, and I am so grateful for God's guidance, care, and protection. Terry has done a great job of leading the ministry over the past 11 years, God continues to abundantly bless, and the ministry is well taken care of.

Juanita and I are now in our 80s. All our children have been so loving and attentive toward us down through the years. Each one has his or her own individual personality, and each one was a joy to raise for the glory of God.

Our adopted daughter, Lisa, was the most challenging, but also had the most difficult start in life. We felt led by the Lord to send her to Maranatha Baptist Academy in Watertown, Wisconsin, for her last two years of high school. Lisa was gloriously saved at a Sliverstate Youth Camp and has faithfully served as the pianist in her Bible preaching church for many years now. Lisa is a very talented woman and married to a wonderful Christian young man that used to attend Juanita's Sunday school class, and together they have raised three children for the Lord.

Gary has always been very faithful, staying by our side, and ready to work, help, or serve. It was Gary that kept the WAE airplane maintained in the beginning. He married a sweet Christian girl that he met at Bible college. They raised four children, two girls and two boys, to love the Lord. Gary presently works as an executive pilot and mechanic out of Alton, Illinois. His wife works as secretary for the church and Christian school, and also plays piano for their church.

Cindy was the studious one and the only one that graduated from Bible college. She loved to sew and became an excellent homemaker and seamstress. Cindy married a young man from Bible college; together they raised five children for the Lord. She and her husband presently serve at Appalachian Bible College in Beckley, West Virginia.

Gerald also had some difficulties to overcome. It took some time for Juanita and me to effectively learn how to work with Gerald, enabling him to reach his potential. Gerald has become a real blessing and asset to the Shepherds ministry, while training other students in horticulture. He is a hardworking, faithful man, who is loved by everyone who knows him.

Sharon is a red head—need I say more? Sharon has always been by our side (whether we wanted her to be or not) and faithful. Sharon married a young man from Park Rapids, who was the quarterback for the football team; they attended Bible college together. They raised two sons for the glory of God. She has faithfully cared for us as we grow older.

Our children have blessed us with 14 grandchildren and 14 great grandchildren, to date, and we love them all! Our desire is to occupy until Jesus comes; but we are yearning for our long-awaited home!

Bob and Juanita

Appendix A
Heaven or Hell?

Dear reader, have you ever considered your eternal destiny? That is the most important question you will ever face in this life. The Bible is God's personal message to each one of us and contains all you need to know to be assured of a home in heaven. Proverbs 14:12 says, *"There is a way which seemeth right unto a man, but the end thereof are the ways of death."* This simply means that our own way may seem right to us, but it is going to result in death. How can this be?

The Bible clearly teaches that all men are sinners. Romans 3:23 says, *"For all have sinned, and come short of the glory of God."* The Bible also teaches that because of our sin, we are under the penalty of death. Romans 6:23 explains that *". . . the wages of sin is death . . . ."* That death is not just a physical death but also a spiritual death, or separation from God. Isaiah 59:2 says, *"But your iniquities have separated between you and your God . . . . "*

However, the wonderfully good news is that God sent his Son, Jesus Christ, to die in our place, to pay our sin debt, and to set us free from the death penalty of sin. The Bible says in Ephesians 2:8-9, *"For by grace are ye saved through faith; and that not of yourselves: it is the gift of God: Not of works, lest any man should boast."* God's enabling grace is available to anyone and everyone who is willing to respond to God's call. God asks us to simply believe what he says in his word.

Only the Lord Jesus Christ can save you! Acts 4:12 says, *"Neither is there salvation in any other: for there is none other name under heaven given among men, whereby we must be saved."* And then in Romans 10:9, *" if thou shalt confess with thy mouth the Lord Jesus, and shalt believe in thine heart that God hath raised him from the dead, thou shalt be saved."* Be assured that nobody else and nothing else can save you—not yourself, not your money, not your church, not your good works—nothing!

So, how then can you be saved?

- Acknowledge that you are a sinner. Romans 3:10 says, *"As it is written, There is none righteous, no, not one."*
- Believe the gospel—a loving God sent his only begotten Son, Jesus Christ, to die on the cross as an atonement for your sin. He was buried, rose again in victory over sin and death, and gives eternal life to those who believe in him. John 3:16 says, *"For God so loved the world, that he gave his only begotten Son, that whosoever believeth in him should not perish, but have everlasting life."* Romans 6:23 reminds us, *"For the wages of sin is death; but the gift of God is eternal life through Jesus Christ our Lord."*
- Repent, turn from your sin, and trust God to save you. The Bible says in Acts 17:30, *". . . God . . . now commandeth all men everywhere to repent."* God also says in Mark 1:15, *". . . repent ye, and believe the gospel."*
- Invite Jesus Christ into your life to be your personal Lord and Savior. Romans 10:13 says clearly, *"For whosoever shall call upon the name of the Lord shall be saved."*

You could pray something like this:

Dear God, I know I am a sinner and in need of forgiveness. I believe that Jesus Christ shed his precious blood, died, and rose again to pay the penalty for my sin. I repent and turn from my sin, and I now ask Christ, the risen Savior, to come into my life as my personal Lord and Savior.

If you have repented of your sin and put your trust in Jesus Christ and his finished work on the cross, you have just begun a wonderful new life with him—you have been born again! Please let us know of your decision by dropping us a note. We want to rejoice with you, pray for you, and help you with good Bible study material. Write to us at the address on the back cover. We would love to hear from you.

Appendix B

Letters

I wish that we could tell the story of each mission trip we have flown, name every one of the wonderful pastors and godly men and women that we have had the great privilege of working with and serving, and share each letter we have received from those who accompanied us on mission trips, but if we did, you couldn't pick up the volume! Here are just a few letters to challenge and encourage your heart, dear reader.

****

I wanted to write and say thanks from the depths of my heart for the recent mission trip to Mexico. I do not believe my ministry at home or my burden for missions and missionaries will ever be the same again.

I have now a greater respect for missionaries in Mexico than I've ever had in my 28 years of pastoring. I also have greater compassion for the people in Mexico and here at home. I realize that if people can live in such poverty and lack of spiritual influence just across the borders from the U.S., unless there comes a great revival in churches in America, we could be where they are.

The acceptance of the gospel by people on the street, in the churches we visited, in the juvenile detention center, and in the church in San Juanito, with no building or regular pastor; the homes on the side of the hill in Monterey; the intersection in Nuevo Laredo, where tracts and a few bags of clothing were given—all have broken my heart for souls.

I, at my age, could not endure the heat and the things our missionaries endure there, but I can pray for your work that other pastors might have the experience that I had. I can preach with more fervor that God would call young men and women into the ministry. I commit myself to do a better job at home and abroad. I would go back in a minute if I thought it could encourage, inspire, or reach others.

 Keep up the good work. I will daily pray for you and the trips you take with other pastors.

—Pastor T. J. Smith

* * * * * * *

Thank you for the tremendous trip to Mexico. While I have had a lot of contact with missionaries and mission projects, this trip was very special. The mission field is more real when we are standing right there with the missionaries. I really appreciate your professionalism in all phases of the trip.

 There is new excitement for missions among the people who went on the trip. It is already affecting others among our people.

—Pastor Robert Crane

* * * * * * *

Having worked with Bearing Precious Seed Ministries for several years, it has been my privilege to print and help distribute God's Word. Many reports have come back about how souls have been saved and how eager people have been to get hold of the Word of God.

 The last two years have afforded me experiences that will never be forgotten. I have had the honor to fly with Wings as Eagles into the interior of Mexico and help with the distribution of the Word of God and hold evangelistic services. All the reports I have heard never prepared me for what I was about to witness: gracious people who actually thank me for bringing them God's Word. Multitudes of people coming out to the special services. Dozens of souls saved. Loving people who count it a privilege to have an American in their home for a visit and thanking us for thinking enough of them to come all the way down there to bring them the Good News of Christ.

Traveling down to the mission fields of the Mexican interior has given me a whole new perspective as to what missions is all about. I would recommend it for most everyone, especially for the high school graduate about to go into college; it would be a lifechanging experience that would surely strengthen their commitment to the Lord's work.

—Burnie Ecklund

* * * * * *

I want to express to you personally and to the Wings as Eagles' family my appreciation and gratefulness for the opportunity to go with you to Honduras to see the work of Brother Bob Tyson and the Good Samaritan Baptist Mission.

I am unable to adequately express to you what it did for my heart, my vision, and my understanding of the cause of worldwide missions. All I can say is that over and over on the trip God's Spirit used the people, the places, and the experiences to make a profound impact on my soul. I better understand the need and meaning of compassion, love, kindness, and duty. Because of your vision for missions my heart was touched. I know that now I have a new understanding of the fields that are "white unto harvest" and of the need for laborers. I will be able to urge greater sacrifice of our people concerning their giving for the cause of Christ. I believe I will be a better pastor here in Park Rapids and a better Christian for having had the opportunity to travel with Wings as Eagles to Honduras.

May God be pleased to increase your ability to do even more for the cause of Christ.

—Pastor Larry Bronkema

* * * * * *

Since the return of our recent trip to Monterey, I cannot escape the vividness of those memories. Again and again I see the hungry Mexican faces so anxious for the truth of God's precious Word.

Seeing our first service on Tuesday night in the barn, with the tractor, beans, pigeons, etc., and nearly fifty people, many of them standing for the entire service, would not have happened in America. The Holy Spirit is ready to work anywhere!

Thank you, precious brother, for the safety and concern for our every need and for the zealous and humble leadership, which made this trip extra memorable.

—Pastor John Correll

Appendix C
WAE Trip History 1984—2010

Over the years, Wings As Eagles has flown mission trips for a variety of purposes: delivering Scriptures, Scripture distribution, assembling of Scriptures, construction projects, vacation Bible schools, Bible camps, canvassing and soul winning, conferences, missionary training, and medical and mercy flights.

April 1984	Veracruz, Veracruz, Mexico
	Missionary Don Rogers
February 1985	Oshkosh, Wisconsin—Pastor Howard Nelson
November 1986	Prince Albert, Saskatchewan, Canada
	Pastor Raymond Dell
December 1986	Bowie, Texas—Missionary Don Frazer
March 1987	Prince Albert, Saskatchewan, Canada
	Pastor Raymond Dell
April 1987	Tampico, Tampico, Mexico
	Missionary Paco Guerrero
April 1987	Veracruz, Veracruz, Mexico
	Missionary Don Rogers
April 1987	El Paso, Texas—Missionary Carlos Demarest
May 1987	Puerto Lempira, Gracias a Dios, Honduras
	Missionary Buck
July 1987	Bowie, Texas—Missionary Don Frazer
September 1987	Veracruz, Veracruz, Mexico
	Missionary Don Rogers
October 1987	El Paso, Texas—Missionary Carlos Demarest
August 1988	Camp of the Woods, Ontario, Canada
	Missionary Garland Cofield

May 1989	Jimenez, Chihuahua, Mexico	
	Missionary Lanny Ashcraft	
May 1990	Buenaventura, Chihuahua, Mexico	
	Missionary John Dunbar	
March 1991	Monterrey, Nuevo Leon, Mexico	
	Missionary Tommy Ashcraft	
April 1991	Guerrero, Chihuahua, Mexico	
	Missionary Jerry Collins	
April 1991	Monterrey, Nuevo Leon, Mexico	
	Missionary Tommy Ashcraft	
September 1991	San Marcos de Colon, Choluteca, Honduras	
	Missionary Bob Tyson	
December 1991	Monterrey, Nuevo Leon, Mexico	
	Missionary Doyle Johnson	
February 1992	Monterrey, Nuevo Leon, Mexico	
	Missionary Tommy Ashcraft	
March 1992	Monterrey, Nuevo Leon, Mexico	
	Missionary Tommy Ashcraft	
March 1992	Oremex Ministries, McAllen, Texas	
	Missionary Valente Hernandez	
April 1992	Guerrero, Chihuahua, Mexico	
	Missionary Jerry Collins	
May 1992	Guerrero, Chihuahua, Mexico	
	Missionary Jerry Collins	
September 1992	Monterrey, Nuevo Leon, Mexico	
	Missionary Tommy Ashcraft	
October 1992	Monterrey, Nuevo Leon, Mexico	
	Missionary Tommy Ashcraft	
October 1992	Guerrero, Chihuahua, Mexico	
	Missionary Jerry Collins	
November 1992	Ejido Constitucion, Chihuahua, Mexico	
	Pastor Ruben Parra	
March 1993	Monterrey, Nuevo Leon, Mexico	
	Missionary Doyle Johnson	
April 1993	Oremex Ministries, McAllen, Texas	
	Missionary Valente Hernandez	

May 1993	Monterrey, Nuevo Leon, Mexico
	Missionary Tommy Ashcraft
August 1993	Uranium City, Saskatchewan, Canada
	Missionary Mark Robertson
September 1993	Guerrero, Chihuahua, Mexico
	Missionary Jerry Collins
January 1994	Grand Turk Island
	Missionaries Fred Brethwait/William Randall
	Santo Domingo, D.N., Dominican Republic
	Pastor Alexis Gavins
March 1994	Grand Turk Island and Middle Caicos Island
	Missionaries Steve Williamson/William Randall
April 1994	Monterrey, Nuevo Leon, Mexico
	Missionary Tommy Ashcraft
June 1994	Stoney Rapids, Uranium City, Saskatchewan, Canada
	Missionaries Dave Webster/Mark Robertson
July 1994	Uranium City, Saskatchewan, Canada
	Missionary Mark Robertson
August 1994	Jimenez, Chihuahua, Mexico
	Missionary Lanny Ashcraft
September 1994	Jimenez, Chihuahua, Mexico
	Missionary Lanny Ashcraft
October 1994	Veracruz, Veracruz, Mexico
	Missionary Don Rogers
December 1994	Veracruz, Veracruz, Mexico
	Missionary Don Rogers
February 1995	Barahona, Barahona, Dominican Republic Missionary Mark Grenon
August 1995	Barahona, Barahona, Dominican Republic
	Missionary Mark Grenon
October 1995	Jimenez, Chihuahua, Mexico
	Missionary Lanny Ashcraft
February 1996	Grand Turk Island—Missionary William Randall
April 1996	Cadereyta, Nuevo Leon, Mexico
	Missionary Greg Lambert

April 1996	Monterrey, Nuevo Leon, Mexico
	Missionary Tommy Ashcraft
May 1996	Guerrero, Chihuahua, Mexico
	Missionary Jerry Collins
June 1996	Uranium City, Saskatchewan, Canada
	Missionary Jim Pfaffenroth
August 1996	Grand Turk and Inagua Islands
	Missionaries Fred Brethwait/Steve Williamson
October 1996	Jimenez, Chihuahua, Mexico
	Missionary Lanny Ashcraft
January 1997	Barahona, Barahona, Dominican Republic
	Missionary Mark Grenon
January 1997	Parkersburg, West Virginia—Pastor Mike Lamb
February 1997	Cadereyta, Nuevo Leon, Mexico
	Missionary Greg Lambert
May 1997	Uranium City, Saskatchewan, Canada
	Missionary Jim Pfaffenroth
June 1997	Uranium City, Saskatchewan, Canada
	Missionary Jim Pfaffenroth
June 1997	Yellow Knife, Northwest Territories, Canada
	Missionary Mark Robertson
July 1997	Uranium City, Saskatchewan, Canada
	Missionary Jim Pfaffenroth
September 1997	Uranium City, Saskatchewan, Canada
	Missionary Jim Pfaffenroth
October 1997	Syracuse, New York—Pastor Dave Dunbar
December 1997	Cadereyta, Nuevo Leon, Mexico
	Missionary Greg Lambert
March 1998	La Ceiba, Atlantida, Honduras
	Missionary Nativedad Delarca
March 1998	Cadereyta, Nuevo Leon, Mexico
	Missionary Greg Lambert
May 1998	Uranium City, Saskatchewan, Canada
	Missionary Jim Pfaffenroth
June 1998	Cadereyta, Nuevo Leon, Mexico
	Missionary Greg Lambert

June 1998	Guerrero, Chihuahua, Mexico
	Missionary Jerry Collins
October 1998	Cadereyta, Nuevo Leon, Mexico
	Missionary Greg Lambert
October 1998	Cadereyta, Nuevo Leon, Mexico
	Missionary Greg Lambert
November 1998	Syracuse, New York
	Pastor Dave Dunbar
November 1998	San Pedro Sula, Cortes, Honduras
	Pastor Cardoza
November 1998	Barahona, Barahona, Dominican Republic
	Missionary Mark Grenon
April 1999	Grand Forks, North Dakota
	Pastor Michael Custer
May 1999	Uranium City, Saskatchewan, Canada
	Missionary Jim Pfaffenroth
June 1999	Uranium City, Saskatchewan, Canada
	Missionary Jim Pfaffenroth
September 1999	Uranium City, Saskatchewan, Canada
	Missionary Jim Pfaffenroth
October 1999	Laredo, Texas—Missionary Bill Waldrop
October 1999	Cadereyta, Nuevo Leon, Mexico
	Missionary Greg Lambert
November 1999	Brampton, Ontario, Canada
	Missionary Bob Baker
February 2000	Altona, Manitoba, Canada
	Pastor Raymond Dell
March 2000	Barahona, Barahona, Dominican Republic
	Missionary Mark Grenon
April 2000	Columbia, Tennessee—Pastor Baker
May 2000	Uranium City, Saskatchewan, Canada
	Missionary Jim Pfaffenroth
June 2000	Laredo, Texas—Missionary Bill Waldrop
October 2000	El Paso, Texas
	Missionary Jack Jarvis/Pastor Steve Zienner
October 2000	Winkler, Manitoba, Canada

	Pastor Raymond Dell
November 2000	Laredo, Texas—Missionary Bill Waldrop
April 2001	Laredo, Texas—Missionary Bill Waldrop
May 2001	Durango, Durango, Mexico Missionary Arturo Garza
May 2001	Uranium City, Saskatchewan, Canada Missionary Jim Pfaffenroth
June 2001	Uranium City, Saskatchewan, Canada Missionary Jim Pfaffenroth
June 2001	Yellow Knife, Northwest Territories, Canada Missionary Mark Robertson
July 2001	Uranium City, Saskatchewan, Canada Missionary Jim Pfaffenroth
August 2001	Rogers City, Michigan—Pastor Jeff Dufour
August 2001	Cadereyta, Nuevo Leon, Mexico Missionary Greg Lambert
September 2001	El Paso, Texas; Missionary Jack Jarvis (Originally to Guerrero, Chihuahua, Mexico; Missionary Jerry Collins)
September 2001	Brampton, Ontario, Canada Missionary Bob Baker
November 2001	Cadereyta, Nuevo Leon, Mexico Missionary Greg Lambert
January 2002	Laredo, Texas—Missionary Bill Waldrop
January 2002	Durango, Durango, Mexico Missionary Arturo Garza
March 2002	Farmington, New Mexico Dedication of Navajo New Testament Missionaries Don and Ron Corley
April 2002	Hermosillo, Sonora, Mexico Missionary Don Perez
May 2002	Farmington, New Mexico Missionary Ron Corley
June 2002	Uranium City, Saskatchewan, Canada Missionary Jim Pfaffenroth
June 2002	Fargo, North Dakota—Pastor Tony Scheving

September 2002	Calvillo, Aguascalientes, Mexico
	Missionary Marvin Tobin
September 2002	Laredo, Texas—Missionary Bill Waldrop
October 2002	Brampton, Ontario, Canada
	Missionary Bob Baker
November 2002	Durango, Durango, Mexico
	Missionary Arturo Garza
	(with emergency landing at LBJ Ranch)
January 2003	Laredo, Texas—Missionary Bill Waldrop
February 2003	Laredo, Texas—Missionary Bill Waldrop
March 2003	Farmington, New Mexico
	Missionary Ron Corley
March 2003	Hermosillo, Sonora, Mexico
	Missionary John Perez
May 2003	Laredo, Texas—Missionary Bill Waldrop
June 2003	Great Falls, Montana—Pastor Sheldon Schearer
July 2003	Yellowknife, Northwest Territories, Canada
	Missionary Mark Robertson
September 2003	Durango, Durango, Mexico
	Missionary Arturo Garza
September 2003	La Crosse, Wisconsin—Pastor Bruce Detlaff
October 2003	Brampton, Ontario, Canada
	Missionary Bob Baker
November 2003	Laredo, Texas—Missionary Bill Waldrop
December 2003	McAllen, Texas—Pastor Carl Herbster
January 2004	Hermosillo, Sonora, Mexico
	Missionary John Perez
April 2004	Laredo, Texas—Missionary Bill Waldrop
May 2004	Uranium City, Saskatchewan, Canada
	Missionary Jim Pfaffenroth
June 2004	Alpena, Michigan—Pastor JC Wapplehorst
July 2004	Kenora, Ontario, Canada
	Missionary Cyril Syroteuk
August 2004	Saltillo, Coahuila, Mexico
	Missionary Roger Bowman

January 2005	Hermosillo, Sonora, Mexico
	Missionary John Perez
February 2005	Calvillo, Aguascalientes, Mexico
	Missionary Marvin Tobin
May 2005	Camp Victory, Livonia, Missouri
	Missionary Boyd Halford
June 2005	Uranium City, Saskatchewan, Canada
	Missionary Jim Pfaffenroth
July 2005	Uranium City, Saskatchewan, Canada
	Missionary Jim Pfaffenroth
October 2005	Altona, Manitoba, Canada
	Pastor Raymond Dell
November 2005	Gulfport, Mississippi—Pastor Steve Crane
November 2005	Gulfport, Mississippi—Pastor Steve Crane
January 2006	Hermosillo, Sonora, Mexico
	Missionary John Perez
February 2006	Calvillo, Aguascalientes, Mexico
	Missionary Marvin Tobin
April 2006	Paracho, Michoacan, Mexico
	Missionary Moises Alvarez
June 2006	Alpena, Michigan—Pastor JC Wappelhorst
July 2006	Amarillo, Texas—Pastor Gerald Chadwick
September 2006	Current, Eleuthera Island, Bahamas
	Missionary Dave Spangler
February 2007	Hermosillo, Sonora, Mexico
	Missionary John Perez
May 2007	Uranium City, Saskatchewan, Canada
	Missionary Jim Pfaffenroth
June 2007	Uranium City, Saskatchewan, Canada
	Missionary Jim Pfaffenroth
July 2007	Uranium City, Saskatchewan, Canada
	Missionary Jim Pfaffenroth
August 2007	Pickle Lake, Ontario, Canada
	Missionary Fred Crisco
September 2007	Prince Albert, Saskatchewan, Canada
	Missionary Elmer Bragg

October 2007	Brampton, Ontario, Canada
	Missionary Bob Baker
February 2008	Hermosillo, Sonora, Mexico
	Missionary John Perez
May 2008	Calvillo, Aguascalientes, Mexico
	Missionary Marvin Tobin
July 2008	Grande Prairie, Alberta, Canada
	Missionary Tim Bicha
September 2008	Charlotte, North Carolina (medical flight)
	Missionary Matthew DeLange
October 2008	Sabga, Cameroon—Missionary Tom Needham
January 20009	Sabga, Cameroon—Missionary Tom Needham
February 2009	Calvillo, Aguascalientes, Mexico
	Missionary Marvin Tobin
June 2009	Santo Domingo, Dominican Republic (medical flight)—Todd Stacy
August 2009	Prince Albert, Saskatchewan, Canada
	Pastor Dave Webster
February 2010	Hermosillo, Sonora, Mexico
	Missionary Johnny Perez
February-March 2010	Jacmel, Haiti
	Missionary Mike Pelletier/Pastor CO Grinstead
July 2010	Uranium City, Saskatchewan, Canada
	Missionary Jim Pfaffenroth
August 2010	Prince Albert, Saskatchewan, Canada
	Pastor Dave Webster

Wings As Eagles Mission Air Service

Wings As Eagles Mission Air Service is a ministry of Wyldewood Baptist Church in Oshkosh, Wisconsin. The purpose of Wings As Eagles is as follows:

- To see the salvation of souls and local churches established around the world.
- To help pastors in their "Great Commission" goals by taking them and their people on short term missionary trips, enabling them to have an enlarged vision for the lost and a greater understanding of the missionaries' needs.
- To aid missionaries on the field by supplying Bibles, tracts, and other needs.
- To help missionaries with the physical construction of churches on the field.
- To create within the churches a heart for missions and to encourage their direct involvement in foreign field ministries.
- To see people called by God to the mission fields of the world.

Captain Bob Warinner's CD *The Lord is My Light* is available
from the address on the back cover
while supplies last for an offering of any amount
plus shipping costs of $6.00.

The CD has piano accompaniment and includes the following hymns:
"The Lord Is My Light," "I Walked Today Where Jesus Walked," "What Grace Is This," "The Lord's Prayer," and six others.

Acknowledgements

I owe a debt of gratitude to so many who have made the publication of this book possible. First of all, I must mention my wife Juanita, who has been faithfully by my side through all these 63 years of marriage and has encouraged me and helped me all along the way. It has been quite a journey for her, and I praise God for her! Without her love and faithfulness, the direction of our lives could have been monumentally different. Thank you, my dear Juanita, for making our journey in the service of our Lord possible!

Each one of our children has been so supportive throughout this journey as well. Any one of them could also have been used to alter our life direction, but they, by God's wonderful grace, all grew up to love and serve the Lord and have encouraged me greatly in this writing. Several of our beloved grandchildren have also been a great encouragement in this project.

Two ladies got involved in the editing process early on, and without their expertise, knowledge, unwavering dedication, enthusiasm, and encouragement, I would never have seen this manuscript through to its completion.

Shortly after I started writing, I mentioned to Terry Rushing what I was doing, and he immediately mentioned the name of a friend of the Wings ministry, Alicia Tumchewics from Yellowknife, Northwest Territories, saying that she had some expertise in editing and might be interested in helping. I contacted Alicia, and she very enthusiastically said that she would love to help. Alicia has been such an encouragement throughout this project, and I thank God for her and the many, many hours that she has dedicated to this.

One of our own Bart Case, has a wife who is an English major, a graduate of Bob Jones University, and loves to do editing. I was really hesitant to seek her help as she is busy. However, as we progressed into the work, it was recommended that I seek another qualified set of eyes to help in editing. I contacted Nancy, and she also enthusiastically agreed to help. These two ladies have kept me on course and have encouraged me and helped me beyond my ability to describe. Thank you, Alicia and Nancy, for your incredible contribution, and may our Lord bless you exceedingly, abundantly above all that you could ask or think!

Others who have had a part and contributed to one degree or another include Bill and Ethan May; Gary, Dan, and Michael Warinner; Tim Carpenter; Terry Rushing; Sam Coman; Joann Borlee; Nathan Borlee; Bethany Seidel; Julie Nye; and Chad Smith. GLORY TO GOD and SHAME ON THE devil, for great things HE hath done!

Our beloved daughters, Cindy and Sharon got deeply involved in bringing this project to a conclusion. I praise God for them and for the deep love they have and demonstrate toward their parents.

Thank you and God bless you all!

www.ingramcontent.com/pod-product-compliance
Lightning Source LLC
Chambersburg PA
CBHW051047160426
43193CB00010B/1095